ON THE GROUND FLOOR OF HEAVEN

ON THE GROUND FLOOR OF HEAVEN

by
REUEL B. PRITCHETT
WITH
DALE AUKERMAN

The Brethren Press, Elgin, Illinois

ON THE GROUND FLOOR OF HEAVEN

Printed in the United States of America

Cover Design by Ken Stanley

Library of Congress Cataloging in Publication Data

Pritchett, Reuel B, 1884-
On the ground floor of heaven.

1. Pritchett, Reuel B , 1884- 2. Church of the Brethren—Clergy—Biography. 3 Clergy Tennessee Biography. 4. Tennessee—Biography I. Aukerman, Dale, joint author II. Title.
BX7843.P73A34 286'.5 [B] 79-543
ISBN 0-87178-666-4

Published by the Brethren Press, Elgin, Ill.

PREFACE

In September 1952 I went to New Windsor, Maryland, to enter a training unit of Brethren Volunteer Service. The theme for that first of nine weeks was church history. The guest leader, straight from Tennessee, was a sixty-eight-year-old preacher I had not heard of before, Elder Reuel B. Pritchett. I had come into this from a prestigious seminary and listening to well-known professors. But Brother Pritchett immediately became for me the most memorable, captivating, and colorful teacher I had ever had.

Brother Pritchett always stood out in his plain garb. At Church of the Brethren Annual Conferences there would be each year a very few others in the dark garb, almost all from Eastern Pennsylvania; but the substance and abiding significance of that past was centrally and most vividly present in one aging brother—Reuel Pritchett.

I find it stirring to ponder photographs, especially group pictures, of church leaders of the first half of this century. One sees in those faces an austere intensity, an intimation of faith's fire within; the pictures are so different from those of their successors. Some of those men, quite somber in photograph, were full of rambunctious humor and at times almost playful, yet holy, spontaneity. For me, Reuel Pritchett was the last survivor from these. He was a remarkable left over, not so much in garb or in what he stood for, but as living out still in our midst for the third quarter of the twentieth century the otherwise vanished style and substance of that earlier type leadership. The spirit of an era already ended continued in him.

Reuel Pritchett was for me an extraordinary man, one of the greatest I have had a personal friendship with. I have known no equal of his in picturesque oral command of the English language, no equal in story-telling, no equal for coming forth with a continuing flow of memorable insights and comments.

The warmth and affection of our father-son-like friendship

grew through two decades until his death. I took many pages of notes already from his lectures in BVS training. But a long cherished intention was fulfilled in February 1964. While on a peace preaching mission to the Brethren congregations in Tennessee, I spent a week with Brother Pritchett in his home near White Pine. I had him tell of his life, I asked a question now and then, and all the while an old tape recorder was turning. I came away with about twenty hours of recordings (which later went to the Reuel B. Pritchett Museum in Bridgewater College, Bridgewater, Virginia). The best parts of these recordings I transcribed and then ordered into a chronological and thematic sequence.

It seemed so right to let the account remain in Brother Pritchett's own words; for who could put it into better words than his? There was the problem of his oddities of speech and grammar. He loved life and he loved living out the uniqueness of who God enabled him in endowment and holy spontaneity to be. His non-standard grammar was not because of lack of education. It was a part of the vivid whole of who he chose to be. Nearly everything has been kept in his exact words except for an occasional change where his grammar would on the printed page seem to have a crudity that was not there in his speaking.

The manuscript came near getting published soon after its completion in 1965. Various problems dashed one possibility after another. In 1977 I showed the manuscript to Brethren historian, Don Durnbaugh. He was chuckling over it for the next hours, said it must be published, and took up its cause. And Brother Pritchett's story finally appears.

It is a book for all ages. Even when our children were quite young, they loved having the stories read to them. Several editors who fell in love with the book have reported the same for their children.

My deepest impression out of the week in 1964 and my final times with Brother Pritchett was that of his intense reckoning with death. Boswell records that when Dr. Warren said to the dying Samuel Johnson, he hoped he was doing better, Johnson replied, "No, sir; you cannot conceive with what acceleration I advance toward death." Through many years, Brother Pritchett sensed something of that acceleration. Like Johnson, he trembled at the prospective awesomeness of the Day of Judgment. He was often overwhelmed with how much he still had to do and how short the remaining time for doing it might be. Much of what he was so absorbed in during those last years—files of clippings needed to be set in order, scrapbooks on various themes had to be completed, stacks of miscellaneous materials awaited his going over them—

was, I thought, rather marginal to God's mission for him through nine decades on earth. My hope, though, is that this book, derived from a parenthesis in those activities, gives expression to the heart of that mission and comes as a continuation of it.

Dale Aukerman

A BRIEF BIOGRAPHICAL SKETCH

Reuel B. Pritchett

Reuel B. Pritchett was born in Washington County, Tennessee on April 13, 1884 (Easter Sunday) to Rebecca Ann (Bowman) and James Alfred Pritchett. In 1908, five years after his graduation from Boones Creek High School where he was an active member of the debate team, he was elected a minister by his home church, the Knob Creek Church of the Brethren. He entered Daleville College in Virginia that same fall to prepare for his lifetime vocation.

In 1911 two major events were accomplished in Reuel Pritchett's life: he married Ella Poff of Christiansburg, Va., and he purchased a fruit farm about a mile from his parents' home in Tennessee. Here the Pritchetts subsequently reared their four children.

Pritchett's career as a free minister was illustrious. He was a popular evangelist and was instrumental in establishing a number of churches in East Tennessee, serving as pastor of the French Broad congregation for 25 years. He was moderator of the Southeastern District of the Church of the Brethren on six different occasions, and his presence and clearly expressed convictions were always anticipated at the Church of the Brethren Annual Conferences. In 1956 he was recognized as Rural Minister of the Year for the State of Tennessee.

The Reuel B. Pritchett Museum at Bridgewater College, Bridgewater, Va., was made possible by the donation of a larger personal collection Pritchett himself had made over his lifetime. He also collected and was interested in writing about many historical incidents which occurred in East Tennessee.

Following World War II, he traveled to Europe as a representative of the Church of the Brethren in its relief work in Europe.

At the time of his death, April 2, 1974, at the age of 89, Pritchett was a resident of Asbury Acres, Maryville, Tennessee.

A more complete treatment of the life of Reuel B. Pritchett can be found in his biography, *Reuel B. Pritchett, Churchman and Antiquarian*, by Roger E. Sappington, Bridgewater, Virginia.

CONTENTS

Chapter One

AN INKLING OF A CALL

Father had a big pictorial Bible. We children weren't supposed to handle it; but when Mother and Father would be away, I'd carry out that old Bible, rest it on the bottom of a chair, and open it up. We'd have church. The other three children were younger, and I always did the preaching. I'd stand by, pound on the Bible, and preach out. My sisters would have their dolls in the meeting. John would bring the cat and hold him. When we prayed, we got on our knees. The dolls readily went down on their knees, but John always had a hard time getting the cat to pray.

We had funerals too. If a chick or kitten died or a rat was dead or we found a dead bird, we had a service. We'd dig a grave in our children's graveyard and wrap the little corpse in a rag or paper of some kind, lay him down in the middle and fold it around him gently. We'd preach and pray. I would describe this poor little bird who would never fly away any more; it had to die and leave its mother. And we'd have Father and Mother's old hymnal without any notes. I knew a few of the hymns, I'd heard them sung so much; and even when I couldn't read, I could rehearse them anyhow. We would deposit the dead, put some little sticks in to hold the dirt up off of its body, line that with a piece of paper, cover over the dirt, and set up a headrock. The girls would strew wild flowers from nearby. We'd sing and have a dismissal service.

One of the pictures in that old Bible which made a great impression on me as a small boy was the scene of Korah, Dathan, and Abiram. A wide gaping crack split open the earth, and these men with all their families and all their appurtenances were dropping into it. One of them clasped a handful of grass and another, a rope, their eyes about to pop out. There they fell pell-mell down to hell. Once in a while I'd tiptoe in and gaze at that picture. I wasn't acquainted with the story, but it impressed me profoundly.

Later I found out how Korah, Dathan, and Abiram had set up a spurious worship among the children of Israel. The Lord told Moses, "You go down there and tell 'em to get out of the tent."

But they put their thumbs behind their vests and jeered: "This is our business. We're not a-goin' out."

Moses went back and told the Lord how disappointed he was. And the Lord said, "You take your hosts and get up on the hillside and let me handle Korah, Dathan, and Abiram.'' The people that heeded Moses was still scrambling up the slopes when the earth behind them split wild asunder and they shuddered at the fading cry of those who plunged into that bottomless chasm. I've preached on the story many a time through the years.

Close to our grade school, at the foot of the Master Knob, was a cave that led under the ground. It was an unimproved cave and sometimes when water accumulated in there you couldn't get very far back. But if it was anything like dry, you could venture along for a couple hundred yards. On bad days, snowy days, rainy days, and cold days, we scholars would resort to the cave for protection. The girls didn't come any further than the mouth of the cave. It wasn't good etiquette for them to. We boys'd do a little digging and find arrowheads, chips, fire coals, and bones from the times when the Indians had inhabited that cave.

But while the crowd of scholars was in there and nothing else to do, then would be an opportunity for somebody to take charge and lecture or preach. I did that on occasion. They'd all listen, though some of the boys would laugh and make fun; but I didn't pay any attention to that.

I was raised under the old school in the Church of the Brethren, and one of my pet themes was baptism—triune immersion. I knew it purty good because I had heard so much on the subject. So I'd quote the boys Matthew 28: ''baptizing them in the name of the Father, and of the Son, and of the Holy Ghost.'' I would instruct and explain and exhort that this was a three-act baptism. Some of the boys was Methodist and sprinkled; others were Baptist and had a single backward action; some belonged to various churches. They argued hard for their views, but I'd try to hold my position. The boys kept calling my church ''them Dunkards.'' They didn't know, and I didn't know back then, that ''Dunkard'' is a corruption and we were really Dunkers—from ''dunk'' meaning to dip, plunge, immerse, put under. Occasionally the teacher would slip up near the cave entrance, and I'd be preaching to the teacher.

In 1888 came the deepest snow that was ever recorded in Tennessee. It was two or three weeks falling and building up. The snow everywhere was over the fences and froze so hard you could walk on top. You'd do fine walking a piece and then break down in. For a time the roads weren't broke, and you couldn't get through with horses. Father made a long-handled rake and pulled the snow down off of the roof so it wouldn't crush the house in.

But wood got scarce. Father had two huge chinquapin oaks that he wouldn't have taken anything for. One of them is there yet, over six feet through, clinched on the solid rock by the spring, surely the largest tree in the county. But Father shoveled a path from the house to the other chinquapin oak; it was the closest thing for wood. He shoveled out paths in four directions longer than the tree was, the one back to the house, and three other ways. The snow where he made the paths was higher than his head. Father haggled that tree down with an axe. He chopped on it almost all day. In the evening Mother went out and they stepped the distance how far she'd have to stand back not to get hit, for there was no telling which way it might fall since it was haggled out all around. The white clouds and the ground white, just looking up from under the tree there was nothing to compare as to whether it was teetering or not. But Mother could occupy a strategic spot and shout to him which path to run down. The great oak swayed and fell. I was a boy of four and saw it.

I was born Easter Sunday, April 13, 1884. My father was a carpenter by trade. He would ride horseback to Johnson City four miles, work ten hours at ten cents an hour, and make a dollar a day on which to raise his family. Father was a short, strong, spare-made man.

It was no unusual thing for us children to get up of a morning, and Mother wouldn't be at home: nobody to fix breakfast. Daddy couldn't cook; he couldn't boil water without scorching it. And we'd inquire about Mother. He was a little delicate about telling us, but he'd finally say, "She's gone up to Uncle Daniel Bowman's. Aunt Sue is sick."

We were uninformed about the whole process, but Mother was a midwife. They came after her on birth occasions many and a many and a many a time. They'd come after her on horseback, and Mother'd ride along horseback. There was hardly a fortnight all the prime of her life but what she was called on. She was famous for delivering babies. For this she never got a penny in all her lifetime. It was a call with her. She loved to do it. The same thing was in her that has been in me with preaching.

Sometimes it was late in the night before Daddy got back from his work. If it was awful bad, he might remain in the city after working ten hours and not be home overnight. Mother would put us children all to bed, maybe say a bedside prayer with us. Before I'd go to sleep, I could see Mother blow the old oil lamp out, kneel by the bed, and break right out in prayer. She no doubt thought we were all asleep, but I was a-hearing her drowsingly. She'd name Daddy, who was trying to make a living; name Reuel, that he might grow up to be a useful man; name John and Claudie and Lizzie and her father and mother; name them over one by one. She'd talk it all over.

As far back as I can remember, I had an inkling or a call to be engaged as a Dunker preacher, a minister in the Church of the Brethren. I don't remember how far back and how little I was but what I had that inkling. Mother had a strong interest in the church and in the ministry. Either I was born with it or she prayed it into me, one or the other. On one occasion I had such an impression of being called to the ministry that I asked my parents if we shouldn't have prayer—and me a boy maybe ten years old. I don't guess I prayed out loud, but we had prayer.

Mother was from an old Brethren family, but Father was Baptist. The Pritchetts were Irish from Dublin. Great-grandfather Singleton Pritchett was a thoroughbred Irishman, but he married a German—though not German-born—as did my grandfather, Father, and myself. Mother was in the church when Father and her were married. Daddy never got in the church for a while. As a little boy four years old I saw them baptize him. I stood by an old plank fence and watched with profound interest as they put him under the water. That scene fastened itself in my cranium, and I see it just as plain as if it was yesterday. The fact of the matter was, I halfway thought they was a-drowning Daddy. But they had baptized some others first, and it didn't create any scene with me.

Uncle George Bowman was one of the leading men of the Brotherhood and an elder of the old Knob Creek church. He was a distant relative to my mother, about a second cousin to my grandfather. He was a great scriptorian; any common scripture, like anything in Matthew, Mark, Luke, and John, was right at his fingers' tips. I've seen him give chapter after chapter in a series of meetings and never once look down at the Bible. George Bowman was dubbed as "the walking Bible of the South."

Uncle George Bowman was a masterful preacher. Before getting up to speak he was susceptible to scratching his head and making the awfulest snurly face. I don't know whether he was trying to think or what. He wore tolerable long hair and was a one-eyed man, though you couldn't tell it; both eyes looked good. When Uncle George'd go to stress a point on doctrine, he'd call out, "Are ye able to see that? I can see it, and I only have one eye." Once he was preaching, and Daddy was a-sitting up front on the deacons' bench, me beside him, and several other boys my age. We was seven or eight years old, I guess. My eyes were wide, my mouth open, watching him prance there in the pulpit and preach. He made a good strong point and asked, "Are ye able to see that?'' I nodded my head and he exclaimed, ''Even this little boy here is able to see and understand what I'm talkin' about. Surely ye grown-ups oughta be able.'' How that embarrassed me.

Uncle George Bowman was a great traveler, roving far and wide without money and without price. He'd go down in middle Tennessee and up in Virginia to preach, go to the mountains of Kentucky and the mountains of North Carolina, go to district conferences and annual conferences. He never told his wife when he'd be back because he didn't know himself.

Leaving home on a preaching tour he'd come down the road, carrying his grip and overcoat, and stop at my Father's house. He would get a drink of water. If it was dinner time, he'd eat with us. Father invariably offered to send him the next four miles into Johnson City on old Rock, our mule. Uncle George was very gracious and thankful about that. Father would saddle the mule. Uncle George would mount, and I'd get on behind him and hold to him. He'd talk to me all the way on over. We'd get in sight of Johnson City, and he'd dismount on top of Gregory's Hill. He didn't mind the other half-mile walk; and it wouldn't be very safe for me to go on downtown because I mightn't know the way out with old Rock. One time when Uncle George got off of the mule, he reached up, and I fell down into his arms and stood by. He laid his hands on my head, gave a little prayer, and quietly said something that shot me from top to toe: ''Reuel, I want you to be a preacher some day.''

Chapter Two

THE GHOST IN THE ATTIC

My brother John and I were great hands to play ball. We played ball at everything we went to do. We wore our parents' patience out a-playing ball. Whenever they sent us out to do some chore, we'd be passing ball. If it wasn't a ball, we'd have a turnip; if it wasn't a turnip, it'd be an apple or a walnut.

John and I were out in the field. I had the bat, he was a-throwing the ball, and I was a-batting it. Mother had some rotten eggs that came out of a hen's nest; she just walked to the barnlot fence and pitched 'em over. John, instead of throwing me the ball, he tossed me an egg. I hit it, just smashed it. Egg splattered all over me. There wasn't an inch of my body nor my face nor my hair, my clothes or nothing, that there wasn't some rotten egg on. I likely never got rid of that stink. I stunk for a couple of days.

John had the laugh and advantage of me on that one.

Father was a-plowing the garden in the spring of the year; and John and I we were cleaning off ahead of the plow—tomato vines, potato vines, corn stalks, dead weeds—getting everything out of the way so he could plow in it all. There'd been a turnip patch in the garden; they sow turnips in the fall of the year. When it freezes, a turnip'll stand the freeze and won't rot, but it'll wrinkle up and be as tough as a rubber ball. We had the globe turnips, they were round; and John and I, we got one about the size of a baseball, trimmed the head off it and the tail off it, and we was passing ball between times, keeping ahead of the plow, and Pappy a-hollering at us, "Git that garden cleaned off, boys, I'm comin' around there. Git these stalks out of the way"—so forth, so on, he was admonishing us.

Well, we got everything cleared out of the way to our satisfaction, and we went down in the yard and was a-passing our ball. John'd be way over there and me here; I'd throw it, he'd ketch and throw it to me. I backed up and hurled it his direction. The clothesline was right close to him, and that turnip tipped the clothesline, missed his hand, and struck him in the temple. It knocked him flat as a flitter; he just fell like a beef. Oh, I thought I'd killed him. Papa didn't see it.

The turnip knocked him plumb out, but he recovered quick. It wasn't a hard turnip, just a wrinkled, frozen turnip, like a rubber ball.

We had a pet dog, a pug-nosed poodledog. He'd got old and scruffy and maybe ought to have been discarded; but everybody in the family was very much attached to Poodle, as well as myself. John and I, we were scouting around out in the field, with Poodle along. One or the other of us, I don't know which one, proposed that it would be a good time to get rid of the dog. John said, no, he wasn't a-gonna do it. "Well," says I, "I'm not afraid to."

"Yes, ye are," he says. "I dare ye to do it."

Something came on me like a flash, a premonition; I picked up a club and hit the dog in the back of the head and he keeled right over. It killed him as dead as heck. That broke John's heart; he was the fondest of Poodle of us all. He ran back to the house to tell Mother and Father that Reuel killed Poodle. But the alibi I had was that they'd been talking about getting rid of him anyhow because he was old. And I had no idea of killing Poodle, I didn't mean to kill him. I really didn't.

One night a number of us boys was out late strolling home from a corn shucking, and we came by my Father's upper field. Where we boys had to separate, we clumb up on the rail fence and set and talked a while. It was a dark night and no moon.

Father had some nice young cedars trimmed up, high as your head to the first limb; and then they bunched way out. The prize tree was right next to us. The field was full of sage grass—that's grass that shoots up as big as wheat and dies and looks dead. It was well along in the fall of the year and the grass was dry. We boys thought of an experiment: we jumped over, wrung off the sage grass, got up on the fence, clumb the tree, and stuffed that cedar full of the grass, all up in there, just loads of it. Then we struck a match to it. Oh, it burnt vehemently. The moonless night wasn't dark anymore; you could see the time of day by your watch a hundred yards distant. It was a wonderful leaping light. Cedar'll burn if it gets primed; the sage grass primed it, and the tree burnt plumb up. Every limb got burnt off, and there stood the stub trunk just sticking straight up, ghostly like, way on up, and not a limb on it.

Of course Father, he discovered the remains, and he says, "Reuel, what in the world's happened to my cedar tree?"

"I don't know, Pappy, unless the lightning struck it."

He was guessing at the reason purty close, but he didn't whip us.

The chief thing my father would not allow on Sundays was fishing. We'd break over and sneak off fishing anyhow; and I always caught a fish and the fish'd get me caught too. I'd hate to throw it back; I'd bring the fish home, and there you'd been fishing on Sunday.

Father and Mother had rather we didn't play ball on Sunday. But that always seemed to be the best day for "Antony Over." We'd throw the ball over the house and have a bunch on that side and a bunch on this side. You'd throw the ball long and diagonal so nobody'd ketch it. But they spread out and was almost sure to get it, no matter which way you threw.

Part of our house was two stories high and had an attic, which they kept for storage; carpet rags, spinning wheels and reels, old broke-up furniture, and plunder of sundry description they stored back up in there.

On rainy days and cold days and when I didn't have anything else to do, I was pranking with the machines up there, particularly the spinning wheels. I stuck a nail through a thread spool and pounded it fast to the jam of a little gable winder that give some light in. I pulled my wheel plumb back across the room full length, as far as I could get; I'd line it up and turn. The wheel being about twenty-two inches in diameter and the spool just an inch, the spool'd have to turn twenty-five or thirty times to the wheel's once, or more than that I guess it is. Turn the wheel even slow and the spool'd just hum on that nail.

It was in the winter time, and Mother was a-getting supper on the fireplace. Daddy was still away at work. The three smaller children and I were around in the kitchen with Mother. All of a sudden we were confounded to hear the humming of a spool up in the attic.

"Reuel, where are ye?" called Mother. "Ah, I thought ye must be—. Did ye hear that spool?"

"I hear it, Mother."

She'd heard me plenty of times playing with the wheel. But this was night time, and none of us was up there. She looked at me close: "What d'ye reckon that means?"

"I don't know." I was scared pink. The humming quieted down. Mother told us we must've been mistaken; she went on with supper. But then the thing started up again, and some thumps on that floor to boot. I nearly fell over. Mother was terribly upset. The girls were quaking in their socks. It was after dark. Pappy did ten hours in the winter time and rode horseback four miles to get home. And he hadn't appeared yet. It'd be 7 or 7:30 before he'd arrive. We were awful anxious waiting for him. And finally after several more humming and thumping spells up in the attic, Daddy rode in. He went to the barn and fed his horse, put in some hay and corn, came on into the house, and we began to tell him about it.

"Naw," he says, "Becky, that was Reuel."

"No, sir, Alfred," she says, "Reuel was right here in the room with me."

"It must've been one of the other children."

"No, we was all right here."

"Oh well now, ye're just imaginin' things. It couldn't—they ain't nothin' up there. Surely ye ain't that scary, are ye, Becky?"

"Alfred, I wasn't scared. I heard—we heard it a half a dozen times. It wasn't a thing in the world but the spinning wheel driving that spool up there in the attic. And the children was all right here in this room."

"Becky," he says, "I jist don't believe it."

She had him a pan of warm water and he washed. Mother set at the accustomed place, he set at the head of the table, and we children got in on the bench. Daddy returned thanks, picked up a biscuit, broke it open, took a mouthful—and that thing started up. Daddy surged up off of his chair and snatched the oil lamp off of the table. He darted out of this room and into the next, and down the corridor he streaked, Mother right at his heels. I was scared to go with them and scared to stay too. I never will forget how careful Pappy carried that light as he was stalking up to the head of the stairs. And then what would happen when he opened the door into the dark attic room?

Daddy pushed the door back and discovered the phenomena. A spinning wheel has a fork in it for the bearing. The old spinners would take a bacon rind, turn the rind side down and the grease side up, and put it in the forks for the spinnel to run in. I had done that too, and I'd pulled my wheel clear back against the wall. The attic wasn't sealed, and the joist ran lengthways for the ceiling in the next room. My wheel was just on a level with a joist that jutted out from the wall. Rats would scamper along that joist and jump across on the wheel to get at the bacon rind. When two or three rats got on the spokes of the wheel, it'd turn with 'em, throw 'em off, spin the spool, and make it sing. But to add to that, you'd hear the rats flop down off the thing and go buck-jumping across the floor to get back up the wall to get back on the wheel.

When I'm preaching on the Holy Ghost, I go on into detail about how the Holy Spirit is the right name, but the Ghost is a fictitious name; and if you took *Holy* off, *Ghost* sounds very spooky; but precede it with the word *Holy* and that takes the Jonah off. There are plenty of ghosts and plenty of spooks; I haven't been in a neighborhood in my lifetime but what I heard of spooks and spirits and hants and haunts. And if Daddy hadn't investigated that hum, I'd've been going all over the country yet seventy some years later telling about a ghost running that spinning wheel. But we investigated, and any noise or phenomena that is peculiar or mysterious will bear investigation.

I tell that story in every revival I have, if I preach about the Holy Ghost or the Holy Spirit.

Chapter Three

THE SCHOLAR FROM "PRINCETON"

My father went to school before they had any kind of graded lessons. He'd take whatever book from home he could, and the teacher would hear him recite out of that book. Father could barely recollect how they did before that. The teacher sat in a chair next to the big fireplace with a shillelagh in his hand. The folks marched around and round in a circle, spelling out loud, everybody, reading out loud, studying out loud. The teacher fingered his shillelagh, keeping order, making sure everybody was reciting, and maybe once in a while he'd listen to the nearest marching scholar.

I'm a graduate of Princeton, as I often tell people. That slightly needs explanation. My grade school was Princeton. I went there eight years and graduated. We had heaps of fun, and I came out a little less dumb, maybe.

There was a custom that outsiders who didn't belong to a school they were going past might holler "School butter!" That was nothing but a challenge for a fight. In our country it often happened that a great big water-jointed, double-fisted fellow would come by and shout, "School butter!" Anybody that did better be in top shape to get out of the way or be a powerful good scrapper. Well, young Henry Gibson come along by Princeton driving a team. He waited until he got just nearly past the school yard, stood up in the wagon, and hollered, "Schooool butterrrrr!"

That cry no sooner reverberated in the room till every boy of any size—I was too little, but we had ten or more grown men as scholars, even with mustaches—they broke for the door, busted through, and thundered down the steps like horses. Henry, seeing he was in a snap, threw down the lines, jumped the fence, and took through the field, leaving his team in the road. They split right on after him. It was a good two miles to his home and through the woods and through the Knob Creek knobs. But Henry had a head start and got lost in the knobs from them. The boys finally give up and come forlornly back, drove his team up to a wide place in the road and tied them to a post. When school got out that evening and we all ambled home, the team was standing there still. Henry dared not to come back; it wasn't his team nohow. But sometime in the night somebody, maybe the man that owned it, came and got the team. If the horde of scholars would've caught Henry, though, they'd've whipped and tanned him good or ducked him in the creek and treated him cruelly.

We memorized a lot of pieces and gave them at society meetings on a certain Friday night once a month.

"I was born on the Watauga, which in the Indian vernacular means Beautiful River, and a beautiful river it is. I have looked down upon its glassy waters in my childhood and could see a heaven below, and then looked up, and behold a heaven above, reflecting in each other like two grand mirrors. There stand the Roan and the Unaka and the Great Smoky, upon whose summits the storm clouds rise of their own accord. I have seen the lightnings flash and dance to the music of the grand organs of nature and tiptoe from mountaintop to mountaintop." It was a great piece, but that's all of it I can remember. Landon C. Haines composed that as governor of Tennessee.

"The bark that held a prince went down,
The sweeping waves rolled on;
And what was England's glorious crown
To him that wept a son?"

The King of England had a son that was in a boat on the English Channel; the waves capsized the boat and drowned the lad. And there was a poem about it. Mother used to drill me on that and tell me how serious it was.

"The boy stood on the burning deck,
Eating peanuts by the peck. . . ."

The ship in the poem was on fire, and there was racing and turmoil and trouble and distress. But here stands this boy unmindful, disinterested, not caring for nothing, just gobbling down peanuts. Now that's a profound parable.

Just once in my life I made a grandstand play in baseball. The event happened at Boones Creek High School soon before I entered the first year there. It was at least three and a half miles from Princeton to Boones Creek. We ate our dinner and left Princeton at high noon, going not around the road but the nearest cut through the fields. I guess there was a crowd of fifty of us. We had the team and the substitutes, and a lot of people followed along.

The crowd was big. Boones Creek dismissed school and everybody was out on the ball field a-cheering for Boones Creek. We had some cheerleaders too. We were getting along purty good, nip and tuck, two and two toward the end of the game. I was a-playing right field. There was a couple of men on base and a Boones Creek hero knocked the longest fly—I don't know whether I ever saw another fly as long as that one. It was way over my head, and I was way back too. I turned, tore in the direction the ball was traveling. I leaped up the highest I ever did in my life, made a sweeping lick at it, and picked that ball right out of the sky. They cheered for a quarter of an hour. That play gave us the ball game. If the ball'd been one inch higher, I never could've touched it, and we'd've lost the game.

They were saying, "That Princeton, they've got a Ty Cobb down there." But no such thing. It was not a pure unadulterated accident, but it was highly mixed with accident. Wild and high as that ball was, far as I was from it, and poor a player as I was, I ought never have caught it. I played baseball all the rest of my life until I could retire from it, and never did I make another grandstand play to compare with that one.

One episode in grade school I never mentioned to anybody till nigh on to fifty years after it happened. I was out with the boys as usual. We'd go to revivals, corn shuckings, programs at other schools, or be off possum hunting. There was eight or ten of us and we found it convenient to pass along in front of our own Princeton School. Professor I. N. Humphreys was the teacher. I was graduating from the eighth grade. We were close to the closing-out exercises and therefore close to the examination. Of course the schoolhouse was locked. The whole bunch of boys had a hankering to do something a little out of the ordinary and they hit upon getting in the schoolhouse. There was no way to get up to the window; it was high. So they rolled a big stump from way out the road, mounted the stump, raised the window, and got inside. They went to the little table drawer and seized the examination papers out of which they would be examined, including myself. They crawled out the window and rolled the stump back. They walked out the road a piece, raised up an old worm fence-lock, put the papers under the bottom rail, and let it down on them. They couldn't never be found; they were hopelessly gone.

I knew it was a mistake, but I was with the crowd. And there was nothing I could do about it. We hid the papers under that fence-lock and everybody went for home. It was midnight or thereabout. Most of the boys lived in the same direction I did and that was two miles. Every little ways a boy'd go up his lane to his home, and another and another. I had got within a quarter of a mile of my father's house before Alfred Brown, the last boy, angled off home. I let him get up the lane enough. Then I swung around and headed straight back for the schoolhouse. I knew it had been too broad a joke, because the back-kick would be on us: it was our examination. I pushed and shoved and rolled that big stump back to the same window, clumb up, and raised the window. Then I went out the road, pried up that fence-lock and rescued those examination papers, brought them back and put them neatly in the same table drawer they came out of an hour and a half before. I let the window down, rolled the stump back to its same spot, and went home, late in the night.

The next day when the boys, as well as myself, gathered, the exanimation went on just the same as if nothing had happened. The boys couldn't tell whether somebody in the crowd betrayed them or else the teacher had a duplicate. But the thing was, he never inquired. He didn't suspicion that the papers had ever been out of the drawer. And nobody ever knew what had happened until nearly fifty years after that. The last of those boys, before he died I confessed to him. Now I am the last of the culprits left.

In high school our interests kept widening. The girls was on their side and we boys over on ours, and we'd pass notes. Judd Hunt was the teacher, and a solemn man he was. He had the hardest look I ever looked into the face of. But I could be leaning down over my books, write a note, fold it up in a little small wad, get my hand down low, snap the note through the empty row of benches into the other aisle, Bert Wine would pick it up, and Judd Hunt would never see nor know anything. I was so shy with it, he'd've had to be a divine to ketch me. I was passing notes to Bert, and her back over to me, and Paul Bowman, later president of Bridgewater College in Virginia, and the other boys around me was a-looking on. Paul had a world of fun in him; he pushed a little piece of note with a nickel on it over on my bench; and the note says, "This nickel is yours if you'll kiss Bert."

I picked up the nickel and watched my chances. I never smiled. I got up, inched through the barrier bench, keeping my eye on Judd Hunt up at his desk, leaned down to Bert, and smacked her one right in time of books—and got the nickel. And I missed Judd Hunt too; he never saw me. The only unfortunate aspect was, Bert had a toothpick in her mouth. She slipped a note back over to me, on which was scribbled: "Naughty old toothpick." I just nearly snickered out when I read that.

I'm sorry I never kept that note for my files.

Chapter Four

A SACRED AROMA

I was born on April 13, 1884. Mother and Father carried me to Love Feast that fall. Love Feast at the old Knob Creek Church of the Brethren was regular for a hundred years: the first Friday, Saturday, and Sunday in October. The crowds were immense. From every direction they'd come in hacks, in buggies, horseback, and walk. "The Big Meeting," as they called it, was a great time to visit. They'd come long distances, ride horseback thirty miles, to see an uncle or aunt or their kinpeople on a Dunker Love Feast occasion. Lots of people would lodge in the community. The Knob Creek church was provided with sleeping quarters up in the attic. And there was some big homes around where as many as sixty people might stay at one house, sleeping on straw ticks and beds in attic, cellar, and all over.

During the meeting there would be sermons and exhortations and singing; and on Saturday night would be observed the Love Feast proper, to reproduce the biblical description of what was done in the Upper Room: the feet washing, the fellowship meal, the bread and the cup. We on no occasion ever missed going to Love Feast. In my earliest boyhood I sat with Mother at the communion table. I sat and watched them wash feet. That took a good while, and I was always hungry and anxious for them to start eating.

All through my life I've heard people talk about how there is no aroma so savory and delicious as what comes up off of the beef that is cooked for the Love Feast meal. We would be sitting there around the table observing the Lord's Supper with a crowded house of spectators, standing jammed right up till there was hardly room to have the service, and them under the pressure of that beef aroma. It tantalized them; they was longing to have a sandwich or just a taste of it. When the service was over, those old deacons and deaconesses would make sandwiches and hand them toward the spectators, four or five people grabbing at the same sandwich.

Aunt Magdalene Sherfy was a great church worker, a sister to my mother's mother and a famous midwife. Her husband was dead, and she had lost six or seven children in a row with scarlatina, though two girls lived through. She always said there was a peculiar aroma, a sacred aroma, a well-pleasing aroma that went up from the beef at Love Feast into the nostrils of the Lord. And she proved it by two places in the old Bible about God smelling the sacrifices. Well, the best soup I ever did eat I've eaten at the Love Feast—and I've tasted some that wasn't so good. But those old sisters back in my boyhood days, they knew how to make it.

We children could eat the beef and soup at the meal, but of course we couldn't have the communion bread and the cup in the service. Afterwards, though, an old elder might break off for us pieces of that wonderful-tasting, unleavened bread and tell us something about its significance.

I traveled a long distance one time as a boy and forded two rivers to attend a Love Feast at the Pleasant Hill church. A man from way beyond there rode in on horseback. He must have heard a lot of wild stories about the Love Feast, so he journeyed over to see what the Brethren was up to. The Pleasant Hill church had two long tables that run the entire length of the building, one on the right-hand side for the sisters and one on the left-hand side for the brethren. In the old churches they had it that way.

This unknown man, he had a mustache. No Brethren wore a mustache. But nobody knew the stranger, and they thought he might possibly be a Brethren. The house and all around outside was crowded with members and spectators. The singing started and all of the people began to go in. The stranger saw the crowd moving down, down, down. And he went right along with the crowd; he didn't know what he was getting into. They slipped in around the tables, and he did too. There he was, and either direction he'd have to walk over ten or fifteen people's feet to get out to the spectators from the row of brethren he was in.

They had the examination service. And here they come washing feet. He maybe didn't belong to any church, I don't know. But somebody washed his feet, and to keep in the tune of things he washed the next fellow's feet. They passed around the salutation: here come a man a-kissing him, and he kissed the next man. Then they had the *agape* supper with the broth and all, and after that the communion bread and cup. I studied the visitor with lively interest and wondered what in the world he figured he had got into.

There was a custom common with the church to perform what was known as "the visit." It was carried out by the deacons in August and September before the annual Love Feast in October. The Knob Creek church covered a lot of territory. The deacons would meet together and divide up into couples. One couple would take upper Knob Creek; one couple would take lower Knob Creek; another would take Boones Creek; a couple would take Johnson City and Brush Creek. They went from house to house wherever there was a member living; and at meal time they was always invited to take dinner wherever they were.

After the deacons had a few exchanges of friendship, the visit was performed. "Are you still in the faith of the church as was expressed in your baptism?"

And their answer should be, "Yes."

"Are you willing to spend and be spent for the cause of the Kingdom?"

And their answer should be, "Yes."

"Are you in love and fellowship with all the brethren?"

And hopefully their answer would be, "Yes." If there was any "No" answer, then the complaint, whatever it was, should be written down and carried back to the elders' body. And even if they answered only "Yes," they were asked, "Do you have any requests or petitions you would like to send to the council?" If they had one, it was submitted in writing or else written down carefully by a visiting deacon. Shortly after that would be held what we called the visit council, and the queries and petitions and complaints were read and dealt with.

The Love Feast of any Brethren church in those days was the central meeting place for all the country. If there were a hundred Dunkers, there'd be hundreds of spectators. The house'd be full, the yard'd be full, the roads'd be full in ever direction. People would come early to get in the house, and many never got in. Of course lots of people came that didn't care anything about the church. They went to see the crowd and meet relatives and be with the girls and have a good time. There were hundreds of folks did that.

Merchants would come out to the church, and on the hitch lot they would stretch a tent and have what was dubbed as a candy shack. They'd put up some tables and be selling candy, chewing gum, apples, cheese, crackers, cakes, tobacco, cigars, makings for cigarettes. There'd be a wash tub of lemonade: "Two Glasses for 5¢." Later, as times progressed, red lemonade was offered. A boy could walk his girl to a candy shack, treat her to a glass of lemonade, a stick of striped candy, or a slab of chewing gum, and he'd be in high society with her for that occasion at least. And any person that could raise as much as 5¢ could purchase three old Virginia Cheroots. I've seen them cut in halves and six persons walk around puffing tobacco smoke, contaminating the fresh country air where the Gospel was being preached.

That all got to be a nuisance, and there was a law passed in our county that no candy shack could be any closer than a mile of any gathering. So the businessmen would measure the distance from the church door on out the road and right where the mile terminated, they'd stretch their tents. Even then there was considerable traffic and a padded path from the candy shack to the church, droves going and coming.

Out in Kaintucky and the mountains of southwest Virginia they would have a horse traders' lot whenever there was a Baptist association. The delegates of twenty Primitive Baptist churches might be there and maybe twenty-five horse swoppers. We never had that in Tennessee. But on some occasions it was necessary to have the high sheriff of the county out to keep order at the Brethren Love Feast.

The first Dunker that ever attempted to live on Tennessee soil was Jacob Bowman, father of all the Tennessee tribe of Bowmans. He was my great-great-grandfather. Brethren were migrating from Pennsylvania down into Maryland and from Maryland down into Virginia. Jacob and his wife, Susana Millhouse Bowman, settled first in Rockbridge County, Virginia, where the Natural Bridge is now. Susana was born in Germany, and German was Jacob's native tongue.

They were caught in the fever to go west through Tennessee. The story of it has been handed down in several lines of the family. About 1782, Jake and Susana left their seven children behind and headed west with two horses and a Conestoga wagon. With them they had oats, corn, fodder, flour, meal, a side of meat, a rifle gun, a chopping axe, tin plates, a bone-handled knife, a two-pronged table fork, quilts, a change of clothes, and their German Bible. They forded Little River, they forded New River, they forded two or three prongs of the Holston River—there was no bridges—and in the Tennessee wilderness they forded the Watauga River.

As they curved along Sinking Creek in Carter County, they spotted a couple boiling molasses. They stopped, fed the horses, tied them to the high wagon wheels. Jake Bowman strolled down to the creek, talked with the folks, and bought some molasses. After molasses for supper, with enough left over for breakfast, they read their Bible and prayed for their children back in Virginia. They spread the quilts over the fodder in the covered wagon and retired for the night.

As the sun filtered brightly through the forest, Susana called out, "Jake, it's daylight."

"Yeunnnh." He was soon snoring again.

After a while she jobbed him and said, "Jake, I tell ye it's daylight. Ain't ye gonna feed the horses?"

"Yeunh, I'm gonna feed 'em." Over and back to sleep he rolled.

Susana poked him a little harder and said, "Jake, I thought we was goin' west."

"This is west, madame," he says.

They finally got up from the fodder, had a hearty breakfast of molasses and side meat, and fed the horses. They looked around, and Jake made a purchase contract for a piece of land right there on Sinking Creek in Carter County, a little east of where Johnson City is now. Then they headed back to Virginia to get the children. But Jake sickened with typhoid fever and died in Rockbridge County. Susana Millhouse Bowman, brave woman that she was, took the younger five of their seven children and started west again in that Conestoga wagon.

Joseph Bowman, the eldest of the children that accompanied her, became a deacon and a prominent man among the Dunkers. He married the young widow Hoss, built a splendid big colonial brick house, and raised a family. When the Hoss woman died, he purchased a mile square of land on Knob Creek in Washington County and married Christena Beam. He raised another big family of children, out of which has issued maybe forty preachers or more. My mother came through that medium. I'm a great-grandson. In 1818 Deacon Joseph Bowman built a masterful big brick house in the shape of an L on this mile square, and the whole house was two-story, all of it. The partitions on the first floor was removable, and that's where the Knob Creek Brethren had church until 1834 when they built a log church-house chinked and daubed on a corner of his farm. That's the church-house I grew up in.

The Knob Creek church was the oldest Brethren congregation in Tennessee and was considered and called and referred to as the mother church of the district. A brother would emigrate to Knob Creek, write back to Virginia or Pennsylvania that he has found the garden spot of the world, a few more'd come down, and purty soon a lively church was going. The Knob Creek Brethren were sturdy folk, still close to their German origins.

The old Knob Creek church was in its day very conservative. It was always the last church in Tennessee to yield and deflect from anything. We had some old philosophers there that would say "No, no, no" till they died. Back a while before my day it was considered a violation of church etiquette to have a picture made, and a good many of the old Brethren wouldn't. Young people'd slip around, snap them setting in a chair somewhere, and then show them their picture. They just thought that was a sin, for there was one of the Ten Commandments themselves that says, "Thou shalt not make unto thee any likeness," and a picture is a likeness.

Still in my day there was no ties. When a Dunker now and again put on a bow tie, he was talked about and visited for it. I never did wear one. I never wore a tie when I was courting nor on trips nor at expositions or on any occasion; I never had a tie around my neck in my lifetime. I hope nobody will noose me with one when I go to my funeral.

The old Brethren put a lot of emphasis on that scripture verse: "Every idle word that men shall speak, they shall give account thereof in the day of judgment." I've always wondered just how far that should be taken. I'm by nature inclined to tolerate a little levity now and then. Maybe my stories are too much on the frothy side; but I've tried to be strong on the standpoint that a man who's a Christian isn't dragging his face; he enjoys all the cinnamon, pepper, and syrup of life.

The Knob Creek church, nonetheless, was the hub of the whole country religiously. It was the center; all the other churches and denominations regulated their preaching hour and Sunday by what we had done. We had the ups on it: the first Sunday in the month was the Brethren's day. Back then we had preaching only once a month, and the other churches too. We had good crowds, the largest of anybody in the country. People who wasn't Brethren or maybe didn't belong to any church would often refer to Knob Creek as their church and attend meeting there. On Love Feast occasions everybody in the whole community, Brethren and non-Brethren alike, made preparations for feeding and lodging the big crowd. There would be a couple of beefs killed and everybody spoke for twenty pounds or so.

It was a log church, chinked and daubed, sealed inside. The logs showed on the outside. The ceiling wasn't very high. For heat they had two long box stoves with pipes that elbowed together into a big drum and then funneled on up the chimley. There was a side-room built on that had a chimley and a fireplace where they hung the pots and boiled the morsels of meat and prepared the Love Feast. Just back of the church was Knob Creek, which they damned up for every baptizing occasion.

Next to the wall on one side they had a long table that ran lengthways of the church. Behind the table was a bench known as "the preachers' bench" and right in front of it was "the deacons' bench." The deacons set only on the one side of the church. We was really divided: facing toward the preacher the men all sat on the right-hand side and the women on the left-hand side. Up forward on the men's side was the Amen Corner, in spite of the fact that you can't pull an "Amen" out of a Dunker with a corkscrew. It was considered very bad etiquette if a young man brought a young lady in and sat with her on either side—unless they were strangers. Couples from the church separated; she departed over to the women's half and he over to the men's half and fell in with the boys. I remember once seeing the old elder come in the door, stomp his cane on the floor, and exclaim, "Boys, get on your side! Girls, get on yours!" They promptly moved.

Invariably two or three men would preach. They'd be at it for an hour and a half or more. One would open the service and one would preach and one would close. The first brother would line a hymn and read some scripture and preach down through it; that-away he got his say in. He'd set down, and the next brother would really take a text and preach. Then he'd set down, and the third brother would close the service; he'd preach a while.

But there was no advance decision about who was a-gonna preach. With the home preachers, of which there was three or four lived at Knob Creek, it was sort of a gentlemen's understanding that they take it in turns. But our church being the center of the brotherhood of Tennessee, we'd have visiting preachers from a distance, often two or three or four of them. And then the weighty question arose, who's a-gonna preach? Of course our brethren would "prefer one another": extend the privilege to the visiting preachers. But there'd be an argument between the several of them. I've seen them elbow each other, talk about it, pass the word along, line another hymn and sing it while they were deciding. And when one did rise, he might have to throw in a lot of adjectives and other material to give his mind a chance to think.

There were two men at Knob Creek—Peter Bowman, a great uncle of mine, and Coonrad Bashor—that was a good hand to set a tune to the old common meter hymns. Either one of those men could sing common meter and long meter and short meter out of a hymnbook that didn't have any staff nor notes in it at all. I've heard them do it hundreds of times. A strange preacher was at Knob Creek from another congregation. The brethren elbowed each other, got the news passed along, and he rose to open the service. He paged in his hymnbook and said, "Brethern and sisters, we'll sing number 56. It is one of the old Brethern hymns. I've been greatly impressed and touched with it ever since I was a boy." He pulled his specks down to see who could lead it, and he spotted both Peter Bowman and Coonrad Bashor. He was sort of split betwixt two opinions and blurted out, "Long meter, Brother Peter—set the tune, Brother Coon."

There were, of course, no automobiles, and but few hacks; now and then a buggy. For most folks it was either walk or ride horseback. In a church lot like Knob Creek's they had not only hitching racks but also what was variously called an upping-block, a horse-block, or a stile. This was a simple handmade affair: you'd plant four posts about six foot apart one way and four foot another, nail a line of stringers around the top, and floor it to make a platform. At one end you'd have two or three steps coming up. Young fellows would just stick a foot in the stirrup and straddle on a horse. But girls and ladies and others going to church horseback could use the upping-block.

A young man interested in a certain young lady could go to church early and sit out there on one of the two Knob Creek horse-blocks waiting for her to ride up. She'd be wearing riding habits—an overskirt over the top of her nice clothing. It would go down to her toes and come up to her waist. It had draw-strings and was always black; I never saw one any other color. As the lady rides up, the waiting youth steps out from the horse-block, tips his hat, and asks, "Have your horse hitched?"

She nods and smiles her Yes. He takes holt of the horse's bridle and helps the horse side over to the upping-block. He holds the horse carefully while the girl steps off on the platform. He comes around; she loosens the riding habit, drops it down, and steps out of it. The boy picks it up, lays it across her side-saddle, tucks it under the surcingle, and hangs the stirrup over the saddle horn. As he glants off to hitch the horse, she may say, "To a swingin' limb, please." To oblige her he'll try hard to find a suitable branch. If a limb's givy, horses can't break loose like they can from a solid post. The young gentleman returns, takes the lady by the arm, helps her down off of the horse-block, and they go into church together.

After church the process is repeated, except in reverse. He escorts her onto the platform, fetches the horse; she drapes on her over-skirt. He makes sure the horse is sidled close enough to the upping-block so she won't fall down between; he wants to be careful. She mounts and he goes around, takes the stirrup off of the saddle horn, and helps her foot into the stirrup. He hands her the riding switch, tips his hat, and says, "Good day, Miss Mary."

That's as true as Matthew. It happened every Sunday there at Knob Creek. It was an awful good way to get acquainted with a young lady you hardly knew. Good girls and nice girls out of well-to-do families would ride a nice steed to church, and a boy that wasn't quite up, that was more a commoner, if he could oblige the girl at the horse-block, he'd get to speak to her at least. And he might break the ice.

I'd give almost anything to have an upping-block for my museum. When Pappy felled that chinquapin oak during the snow of 1888, he made two upping-blocks, hewed solid out of the trunk. We always treasured them. But after Father died and Mother was dead, John stored them under a house of his that was high off of the ground. Some tenant people took those horse-blocks out from under there, chopped them up, and burnt them for fire wood. I supped sorrow over that. Most folks have no respect for anything old and historical.

Sometimes we had trouble at church. One Sunday morning when we went to church, all the family, Father and Mother and the girls and John and me, we drove the surrey up to the hitch rack. Daddy kept the hitching strops under the back seat of the surrey. He went around, picked up the flap, and one of Mother's old Plymouth Rock hens surged out. She had made a nest in that department and been jostled about in there the whole way to Knob Creek, together with a half a dozen eggs. In great fright and fury the old hen jumped out cackling and squalling. Pappy yelled, "Ketch 'er, boys!" John and I, we had the race of our lives around and under hitching posts, buggies, hacks, hitched horses, and elders. What a commotion it did make among the gathering crowd! We finally ran her down. Feathers flew everywhere, and she squalled till I choked her down. But to cap the stack, a couple of families lived right close by the church, and who was to know but what we boys had caught one of their hens?

I remember hearing my Uncle Joe Sell relate how one Sunday morning he thought he heard something down on Reuben Sellers' place. The two farms joined, with Knob Creek in between. Listening close, Uncle Joe could hear somebody hollering at horses: "Geee . . . whoa . . . turn around there!" It being a Sunday morning, Uncle Joe walked out to where he could see, and sure enough Reuben Sellers was down there in the bottom plowing. Uncle Joe crossed over on the walk-log and says, "Well, Reuben, how're ye gitting along?"

"The ground's plowin' good," he says.

"Well, Reuben—did ye, did ye know it's Sunday?"

"Sunday! No—no, today's Saturday."

"No, Reuben, this is Sunday."

"Now, Joe, it can't be Sunday," and he proceeded to tell why.

"Let's go up to the house and we'll see," says Uncle Joe. Reuben was doubtful enough to unhook from the plow. He led the horses the quarter of a mile and hitched them up in the stable. The two men went in the house, got out the almanac, sketched through the happenings of each day with Reuben's wife; and Brother Reuben finally got convinced that he was out plowing on the Sabbath. Uncle Joe, as it happened, was a Knob Creeker that firmly believed the world was flat and the sun traveled a complete circle around the earth ever day and night, but he was good at knowing which day was Sunday.

Another story I know verbatimly, though it is just flickering on my shore. Whether in my earliest childhood I saw the reality or only the shadow is a question. There was two deacons lived at the Knob Creek church. One was Saul Miller; I knew him well. The other was John Reed. The one had married the other's sister, I don't know which; and the father of the sister and of the brother had divided his property in half and run a straight line right through the old spring so both families could have water. A springhouse was built. The Millers had their milk at one end, and the Reeds had their milk at the other. But springhouse trouble arose. Saul Miller's children would dabble with Reed's milk, and Reed's children dabbled with Saul Miller's milk. The children broke the division, and that fuss got in among the old folks, and then in the church.

Uncle Sam Sherfy was the Knob Creek elder. While the trial was pending, Saul Miller took Uncle Sam home with him and laid out the whole case. Uncle Sam never nodded his head, never said Yes nor nothing nowhere, but listened at it all the way through. He played so awful green about it until Saul Miller said, "Now, Brother Sherfy, ain't I right?"

"I don't know, Saul. I haven't heard the other side."

Well, the trial came up and Uncle Sam was elder in charge. It was tit for tat, just as much evidence and blame on one side as there was on the other. The time to render a decision came. Uncle Sam rose and said, "Brethren, ye'll have to do like I heard about two he-goats once, where there was a walk-log across a chasm. The one goat rammed down the hill on his side and onto the log, and the other goat rammed down the hill from his side and onto it too. The log wasn't by no means wide enough for them to pass on. Both of them was too headstrong to go back. Both goats stood there and waited and balked and stood, until finally one of 'em laid down and the othern walked over him and they both got across."

I always thought that story was original with Uncle Sam. I didn't know the difference for fifty years and never would've probably, had it not been for S.Z. Sharp, an Amish to begin with, who went on to establish Kishacoquillas Seminary, the first Brethren school. I saw him at Annual Conference, when he was ninety-eight, stand on his feet, line a hymn and sing it, read a scripture, and call that vast throng to prayer. A month or two later an automobile hit the back end of his buggy as he was driving down the street, threw him out over the dashboard down under his own horses' hooves, and he was trampled to death. I hinted and negotiated and obtained a huge set of books he had left in the attic of the Colorado Springs church, *The Bibliophile of Literature and Art*. Perusing in it one day, I discovered that Martin Luther told the he-goat story four centuries ago, of which fact Uncle Sam Sherfy was maybe unaware.

Elder Jack Pence was a little fellow but a mighty preacher in Tennessee. He was bald-headed, but he had long locks and he'd comb them up over the top of his head to look like he had hair all over his head. He used to cry, "O young man, what's gonna happen to that soul of yours?" He'd make my hairs stand on end. In those days I heard a number of great preachers—H. C. Early, Andrew Hutchinson, S.J. Smith, George C. Bowman—and many another. When I was eight years old, H. C. Early preached a revival at Knob Creek. I had a little day book and I set down the scriptures he preached on and some of his subjects. But it went along until C. H. Diehl, a Tennesseean, a good man but not a big preacher, he was holding a revival in the year 1900. On the night of January 5, I was strangely moved. He preached a powerful sermon, I thought; it went through me. They sung that hymn,

"I will arise and go to Jesus,
He will embrace me in His arms,
In the arms of my dear Savior,
Though there are ten thousand foes."

It's a masterpiece. It raised me. I walked down the aisle and gave an old saint my hand, and six others with me. That was in the old log church on Knob Creek sixty-five years ago.

(Many a time in preaching I burst out singing a verse of that song right in the midst of a sermon. I'm not a singer, I'm not a musician; I've preached too much in the open and used my vocal cords too strenuously emphasizing and elaborating my text—and auctioneering too—for me to have a gift on the turns of music. But that's a masterful hymn, and I love to sing it.)

There were twenty of us altogether went down into the liquid stream and were baptized. Paul Bowman, who offered me the nickel and became president of Bridgewater College, was one; and my sister Claudie; Jim Wine, who become a preacher. Most of them are all dead. It was wintertime. Knob Creek wasn't froze over; it had a considerable amount of springs. But the water was just at freezing. And hanging down from the bank was big icycles that had frozen on the grass and roots.

The first Annual Conference of the whole denomination I ever went to was held at Bristol, Tennessee, in 1905. It was the third one ever held on Tennessee soil. The first was in 1846 at Knob Creek, and then and there was settled the slave question finally and decisively for the Dunkers, and with no loopholes for slave-holding. The second Annual Meeting was at Limestone in 1860. And in 1905 came the third, held at Fairmount Park on the Tennessee side of the city of Bristol. The park was well furnished with trees, and we had to negotiate with the Bristol authorities for an area to pitch our huge preaching tent and dining tent in. They certainly didn't want us to cut down a single tree. The upshot was, we made slits in the tents and let the trees stick right up through.

There was a solicitation made throughout all the churches in Tennessee for waiters at the table. I volunteered. Knob Creek pooled about fifteen or twenty young folks, Limestone gave a number, and the rest of the churches, and when we gathered, we were maybe a hundred and fifty strong. In the dining tent we had big kittles for cooking. They led the beeves live into the park, butchered them there, and cooked them by the hundreds and hundreds of pounds. Every bite of all the meals was cooked right there. Our coffee pot was a boiler from an engine, about twelve foot long and two and a half foot in diameter. They built a brick furnace under it and fired it high. They'd plop in a bushel bag of coffee at a time and boil it vehemently, bag and all. Abraham Nead, a preacher at Limestone, was in charge of coffee. He kept that boiler a-running three times a day and all day to give drink to those thousands of folks. I've seen them take a bag of coffee out and dump it on a pile, and there'd be bushels of coffee grounds all heaped up. I recall asking Brother Nead how he was a-getting along. He was tired of it and sighed, "I wish this meeting'd close."

Great crowds came to that Conference from all over the United States. Several chartered trainloads journeyed all the way from

California. Seven days they crossed the mountains and crossed the plains; and the trains would sit the whole week through on the side-track at Bristol waiting to take them home. Brethren from everywhere mingled in fellowship. Pennsylvania was there in her best garb and outnumbered any other state. Most of the Brethren were purty plain then still; they wore the plain clothes and very few had ties. Waiting on the table, I loved to hear those Pennsylvania Dutch folk talk and call for food in their Dutch brogue. One day I gave a Pennsylvanian a cup of coffee and he says, "Where's the cow?"

I picked up the cream and handed it to him. He poured cream liberally in his coffee. I set the cream down and picked up the beef and said to him, "Here's the rest of the cow." They laughed from one end of that table to the other. Me just a boy, making such a break as that before all those old brothers.

The Brethren stayed in homes all over Bristol. The whole city was canvassed and everybody listed the number of beds they might spare. Then a lodging committee assigned everybody where to go. The Brethren compensated their hosts at a modest set price, I think.

In those days pickpockets and blackhand were purty common. A number of our sisters staying at a certain rooming house began missing a few of their effects. They got to suspicioning a particular person dressed in the garb but who maybe wasn't a sister. Some more effects disappeared along with the suspicioned person. They got to figuring out that it wasn't even a woman but a man dressed like a sister. That caused quite a sensation among the sisters and brethren.

That conference was the first occasion I ever saw I.N.H. Beahm—Isaac Newton Harvey Beahm—one of the great philosophers of the Church of the Brethren. He was in his prime then, alert, quick, witty, smart personified, well-recognized. He could walk backward as well as I could walk forward. I heard him rare back and call out, "Young man, don't be afeard to wear the beard." I didn't have a beard then.

One night a heavy raging storm swept up, and I.N.H. Beahm was in the tabernacle preaching. The rains smote the tent and whipped it. The trees started picking up the lightning and funneled it right down through the tents. In the dining tent an old woman was standing by a barrel, washing a coffee pot. She got struck by lightning, smashed that coffee pot right on the edge of the barrel, fell on it, and squashed the sides together so it couldn't never be used any more, though I wish I'd've saved it for a relic. She herself laid prostrate for a while, but recovered. A few other people got badly shocked. But the strangest thing was what happened in the main tent as I.N.H. Beahm was preaching about light and darkness. He spoke of the moonlight of the Gospel, and the storm was coming up. He spoke of the glorious bursting sunlight of the Gospel in Jesus Christ, and the lightnings flashed. As he was coming down on the darkness of this world, the electric lights went out. Beahm never hesitated, and there in the dark of the tabernacle and under the pounding rain he preached on and on about darkness. And when he again mentioned "light," the lights came flooding back on. Everybody thought it was providential.

Chapter Five

"A SINGING AT YOUR HOUSE"

Somewhere amid my files is an old *Arthur's Magazine*, published around 1840 or 1845, which carries an article written by a doctor about tomatoes. The doctor verily believed that tomatoes would be a staple food some day.

I've heard my father rehearse how his mother and sisters grew tomatoes for box flowers and referred to them as "love apples." They thought the little things was poison. Young couples would pluck them and as they walked along toss them over their heads and make a wish, which was supposed to come true.

When my Great Uncle Dan'l Bowman, born 1822, was courting his third wife, Margaret Miller of Ashe County, North Carolina, she and other Brethren folk would come to visit the Bowmans. Some of the people in Tennessee were just begining to break through the barrier about tomatoes being poison and were eating them as a kind of food. Margaret Miller, after sampling Tennessee tomatoes with no bad effect, went back to her home in North Carolina and proceeded to pluck a few tomatoes from the flower garden, dipped them in a bit of salt, and plopped them in her mouth. Her sisters ran in the house, shouting to their mother, "Margaret is eating them poison love apples."

In my boyhood we depended largely on what we grew out of the ground. Our gardens and truck patch and barn and crib and smoke house were the major part of our living. We didn't go to the grocery store for much—not even for soap. The art of making soap was a very considerable process. We saved wood ashes the whole year through. During the fall and winter they'd keep the offals of the butchered hogs and the skins off the meat. They'd take the fat off of the entrails they hadn't been very clean with, the maw, the lights, the stomach—then dry and cure it all.

When it was convenient in the spring, Mother would make soap, and I'd help. Like about every farmer of that generation, Father had a big ash hopper, some six feet in each direction, with a roof on top and the sides sloping down into a trough. We'd dump in perhaps twenty-five bushels of ashes into that hopper, dampening them, tamping them down good, leaving a big depression in the middle. Then we'd pour six or eight gallons of water in the depression for a start and keep water running through and out the trough. The lye water would come out purty strong and pregnant with chemical soda ash. But we put it in a big cook pot, built on a fire under it, and kept boiling down the lye water and adding to. We had two tests for whether it was strong enough: if you threw in a hen's egg and it swum the egg, or if you stuck in a chicken feather and it singed all the down off clean to the stem, it was a strong enough lye concentrate to put the grease in.

Then we brought the pieces and scraps of lights and stomach and fat and offals and dumped them in that big kittle of lye. Mother knew, and I learned purty good, about how many pounds of fatty stuff to put in how many gallons of strong lye. You didn't weigh it, but by experience you knew. The lye would immediately neutralize the grease, eat it right up; that's the reason it had to be strong. There'd always be some bones, and Mother'd take the soap paddle and fish them out, clean and white as only the lye could make them. We'd stoke the fire and boil and boil until ever fiber of meat or shred of gristle was thoroughly disintegrated. We'd be all day at it. You couldn't take the soap off while it was hot, so we'd cover it over and let it set till morning.

That made "soft soap," about the density of cold cream. We'd dip it off clean and clear. Anything that wasn't soap, any lye or water or grounds of meat, would be settled down right in the bottom of the kittle. It wouldn't be in the soap. You'd put just a little soft soap in dish water; a teaspoonful would be all you'd need. Or you'd smear a handful onto the clothes you were boiling. If you wanted hard soap—cake soap, the tub soap—you did everything just the same but added table salt, maybe a half a gallon to a kittle and left it set till morning. It would solidify and set up; you cut it in squares just like the tub soap you buy.

A dish common in that generation was lye hominy. Father in the wintertime would put a big kittle on the fire, let the water come to a boil, and dump in several shovelfuls of hot embers. They'd sizzle and steam and turn to lye, and he'd keep adding and keep boiling. After a while he'd pour off the lye, get rid of the grounds, pour the lye back in the kittle, throw in a gallon of corn, and boil it hard right on the fire. The hull would come off, and the little tailpiece that went down to the cob—it would shed that. You had to parboil the corn to get rid of the lye, and there was hominy ready for Mother to slap into a greased skillet and fry for breakfast. You can buy canned hominy now, made commercially in a similar process. But using the embers right out of the fireplace, we beat them to it with the mouth-watering lye hominy of my boyhood days.

In the fall Daddy'd boil a run of apple butter. The big kittle set in a furnace with a stub chimley. He'd make up red clay mud and daub around to get it air-tight. We children'd each enclose an apple in a ball of that mud, clean mud it was, and lay it on the furnace. The fire boiling the apple butter would be roasting the apple. Take the apple up, and you could peel the mud right off, every bit of it. The skin'd hardly be stained; you could slip that off and have wonderful roasted apple.

At Easter we'd take a holey burlap bag, wet it good, lay a row of eggs at the one end of it, and wrap them round and around till there was eight or ten thicknesses on top of the eggs. We'd set a brush pile afire, throw in the sack, and let the brush burn down. The sack was too wet to burn. When the fire died down, we'd fish out the charred sack, rake out our cooked eggs, and relish them down. Maybe they didn't have any real superior taste, but it cooked them all right.

Not long ago I saw the question asked in the newspaper, "What has become of the nail keg?" I had never given it very much consideration. However, I'd saved eight or ten nail kegs and had them setting around. It dawned on me that maybe they're antiques now. So I got together a couple, washed them up, cleaned them up, varnished them up, and put them on display in our museum in the Dandridge Courthouse. And there's been a lot of comment about them; folks say, "Why there's a nail keg. I haven't seen one in ten years."

Now the first use of a nail keg was for horseshoes, muleshoes, nails of sundry sizes, rivets, steeples, and bolts of a hundred shapes and kinds. That stuff was shipped in the kegs, which is really a little wooden barrel with a head in each end and bound together with either wooden or metal hoops. Once emptied in the hardward store, they were frequently used as stools to set around the potbellied stove. They used them for stools, everybody did. Every hardware store around had an overflow of kegs, and the farmer's pick them up and cart them out home. It'd be a gift by the hardware man. Farmers would use them for hens' nests, for bee gums, for soap grease, to store beans or onions or popcorn in, to measure potatoes, and various and divers purposes out on the farm. A mother cat might choose a keg to house her brood in. But nobody has any nail kegs now, and the use of them is gone.

When a death happened in the Knob Creek community, the attention of everybody was arrested. A messenger went around on horseback from house to house. Everybody soon knew and everybody availed themselves of the opportunity to help out. The bereaved house would soon be thronged with friends and neighbors. The bereavement was like a cloud over the whole country.

Twice in my boyhood days the corpse was at our home. The first time was Grandfather David Bowman, my mother's father. Grandmother Elizabeth Garst Bowman was four years older than Grandpa, which was unusual. She lived sixty-eight years, one month, and twenty days, and died. Then Grandpa lived alone. He was carrying a bucket of slop and stepped on a cob. It rolled with him; he fell and broke a hip. He was an invalid for a couple of years. While he was down at my father's house for at least a nice visit, he got bad sick. He lived sixty-eight years, one month, and twenty days, and then he died. His and Grandmother's tombstones stand side by side, and each has the same identical inscription:

"Sixty-Eight Years, One
Month, and Twenty Days."

I was a boy of eight. There was a very pronounced wake in our house that lasted all night. The whole country turned out; everybody came. Late in the evening Mother took us children upstairs to bed. During the night I'd rouse out of sleep and hear them singing down in Grandpa's room.

A body was prepared for burial right in the home where the death occurred. In every community there were men and women that were considered specialists in laying out a body. Such a person was immediately notified and took the lead in the whole process. For the laying out, a "cooling board" was secured, a plank maybe eight foot long and two foot or more wide. They'd rest the "cooling board" on two chairs and stretch the body out on it. The chin was propped up, and a couple pieces of money, placed on the eyelids to keep them shut. A quarter or a nickel would do. When the body chilled, both the chin prop and the coins could be removed.

Even in the towns there were few dealers that carried burial supplies. The coffin—never a casket in those days—was made by some local carpenter. The custom was to go into the woods or a thicket, bring a straight, slim, young growth, and cut it the exact length of the dead body. This would be the measuring stick for the carpenter. The coffin was wide at the shoulders, and a third of the length tapered in toward the head end and two thirds tapered in toward the foot. Everthing was simple, and there was little to buy: some lumber maybe, a few yards of lining for the inside of the coffin, a bit of varnish, and perhaps material for a home-made shroud. A funeral back then cost from $15 to $30.

It wasn't considered good etiquette to leave the family by themselves or the corpse by itself. The neighbors would come in and set up, some in the room where the corpse was and the rest wherever they could find space anywhere in the house. Choirs from different churches came in, and there'd be song service all night long. A choir would sing four or five songs and then yield. Another choir'd sing some songs and another, and so on around in turn. (There was a common saying in the country if a boy was too venturesome swimming or climbing or playing with firearms: "You better be careful, or there might be a singing at your house and you not hear it." I've had that said to me.)

The family where the wake was, they'd have food cooked up and the food brought in. And women'd go to the kitchen and fry and fix and be a-cooking all the time—sandwiches, sweet-cakes, jumbles, meat, most anything—with a stream of folks coming and going, drinking coffee and nibbling sandwiches. Sometimes at midnight or thereabouts the crowd began to scatter, and a few of the neighbors would be canvassed and solicited to remain the rest of the night. As a young man, I stayed myself a number of times. Dark to midnight passed rather quick, but from midnight till dawn seemed a long time in there with the corpse.

Anybody that died before twelve noon today would be buried tomorrow. If they died toward night, it'd be two nights and the second day before they were buried, as a rule. If the death occurred in the evening, people hardly got organized until the second night, so they'd only have the wake then, though somebody would sit up with the body the first night.

Embalming was rare, but we had some local methods for preserving a body through a couple of days. We mixed strong vinegar and salt and kept a rag saturated with it laying over the brow and mouth and face of the corpse. The folks sitting up in the room with the corpse would change that application ever little while. Many and a many a time I've laid a cloth saturated with vinegar and salt across the face of a dead child, a man or a woman, an aged person or a youth. I'd take one off and put another on. That was to hold the color and keep the flesh from decomposing so quickly. If it was wintertime, they didn't carry a fire in the room where the corpse was. People would take turns all night long sitting in that cold. After a half an hour a couple of people would come out where the singing was, and a couple more would go into the corpse room.

The early settlers usually laid out a burial plot on their own farm. George Washington, Thomas Jefferson, Andrew Jackson, Andrew Johnson, they all did that. A man might choose to take his final rest in the shade of a tree he had planted. Lack of roads, clannishment, desire to have the graves of kinpeople close by—all confirmed the practice of having the family graveyard—never called a cemetery. A grave-digging might draw forty or fifty men and boys from over the entire countryside. There were always several men that prided themselves in laying off the grave and locating it just like the family wanted. Working in crews, they would dig down four feet and level up. Then they would dig a catacomb on down just big enough for the coffin to go in, and at the four-foot place there'd be a ledge all around for a board covering that would protect the coffin some.

At the church, one or more ministers would make a talk about the person who had passed on. The obituary was read. Most people were in dark clothes. And for a funeral the women, not just the Brethren women, wore bonnets. The coffin would be loaded back on the wagon, and the procession of walkers, hacks, buggies, and horseback riders would move solemnly toward the family graveyard. We could hear the brakes on the funeral wagon squeaking to hold the procession to a slow gait.

At the graveyard the coffin was opened for the last time. Women wept bitterly; strong men would cry out and send a chill over the audience. A strong pair of check lines from a team of horses close by was used for lowering the coffin. Eight men would hold on to the lines and let the coffin settle carefully down into the catacomb. A man or two would crawl down into the grave and onto the ledge. They'd adjust the coffin and lift it a little so the check lines could slip out. They'd lay the board floor over the coffin. Then the man above would hand down shovels of dirt, very cautious lest a clod drop and make a noise on the wooden floor. When there was a good layer of dirt all over, the rest of the fill could be thrown in quickly, with the men taking turns. For finishing the grave a sharp mound was built up, with the sides pounded down smooth. The immediate family as a rule remained until it was all over.

There came a second time in my boyhood when a corpse was in our house. Our sister Elizabeth—we called her Lizzie—she was a mute, the darling of the family. She could hear, but something was wrong with her vocal cords, maybe from some medicine a midwife gave, and she could never talk. At sixteen she was stricken with penumonee fever. The fever did its dreadful work in three or four days. We children had been taught so much about the angelic bands and the spirit being carried away by the angels to God. Lizzie was in a dying condition all day and until way in the night. Mother was in sobs and tears; Daddy was speechless and humble; the rest of us were standing around and the neighbors and the doctors had been there. If an angel came for Lizzie, I wanted to see him. I would go out into the night and look up for anything strange, as that sister of ours was in the jaws of death. The heavens were vibrant and calm beyond the ordinary.

Chapter Six

IMPROBABLE CHARACTERS

I have often wondered what attractive influence was responsible for bunching together such a variety of improbable characters as was living in the Knob Creek Valley. Through many years I closely observed and relished the peculiarities of the Knob Creekers, of which I rather suspect neither I nor my immediate family was free. I knew and remember every person that lived on Knob Creek from the head spring down the twelve miles to where it empties into the Watauga River: the Persingers, McNeils, Bowmans, Harringtons, Goodmans, Caratherses, Sherfys, Pritchetts, Krouses, Sellerses, Vaughns, Sells, Duncans, Edens, Whites, Fords—and then Buck Hale's mill. I knew every man on the creek or near it; I knew their politics and what church they belonged to, if any. I remember their peculiarities, dispositions, inclinations, deaths, and burials.

We came together for so many things: corn huskings, butter boilings, barn raisings, new ground clearings, hog butcherings, grave diggings, road workings. All the men of the country would come in and put a barn up in a day or two. If a man had a new ground to clear, especially if he was sickly, they'd come in and saw and chop and drag and pile and burn and in a single day have three or four acres ready to plow. Corn huskings were a big event. They didn't husk corn in the field; they gathered it off of the stalk or off of the shock, hauled it in, and threw it in a big windrow near the barn. Then they'd warn in the people, notify everybody, and sixty or seventy might show up. We set crowded thick around that windrow; everybody shucked except the women in at the kitchen, who were a-cooking up a big dinner. Boys'd get to wrastling on top of the pile. At midnight we'd all go in the house for ham, biscuits, mutton, chicken pie, sweet potatoes, gravy, cake, apple pie. At any such community doings the notable characters of the country were unconsciously performing.

You'd have to curry the whole United States to find anybody to match Jake Crumley. He was a clown to look at. Maybe he wasn't actually ugly, but he sure had comical knobby features. Jake would clean up his throat two or three times before he could ever say a word. His voice was thin and wavery; it sounded like the wind a-blowing. He wound around, all around, before he could ever say anything about anything. And then you had to pay close attention.

Jake was purty superstitious in a lot of things. He and his brother, they'd never start plowing on any other day except Monday. If plow weather was in evidence, they'd hitch the team up and go out and plow a round in the field on Monday. Then they could go on plowing any day later in the week if it got dry enough, with no bad luck of any kind. Pappy was handy with tools. He cut hair for people. And Jake wouldn't have anybody to cut his hair except my father.

Jake'd come down of a rainy day; I've known him to show up on Sunday morning. Father would drape his spread around Jake and shear him good. When the operation was complete, Jake always got a broom and swept up the loose hair, careful to get every last one of them. With his precious little pile he'd go out and find a soft place in the garden, bury the hair and tramp the dirt in on it. That was to keep him from having headache after a haircut. He was a curiosity.

Shy, Jake was shy as a fox. Any woman that came around anywhere at all even after he was fifty years old, he would blush and color up and bow his head and back off. But Jakey too had a courtship. The Crumley farm joined the Krous farm, where there lived another set of maids and bachelors. Miss Sarah Krous would walk to the Knob Creek church. Jakey would also walk. Neither family had more than a wagon, and they never thought about taking a wagon the mere two miles to church. After the sermon was over, Jake would shyly station himself close to one of the doors.

There was several doors, but Miss Krous was sure to come out at the door where Jake was stationed. He'd step up to her side and they'd start glanting along, strolling together, talking together for the two miles. That happened on meeting Sunday after meeting Sunday for more than thirty years, and they never married. Jake was a good old guy; he never did nobody any harm. He died, and Miss Sarah Krous died, and they were buried in their respective family graveyards. It was the longest courtship I ever observed.

Bill Melvin had a little mill on down Knob Creek with an undershot wheel where he spent a lot of time. He was a blacksmith and had a shop in the one end. Bill was a bachelor and never had a marital home of his own. He and his sisters, Rhetty and Stacey and Magdalene, lived on the old Squire Jim Melvin farm. The Squire had been a man of affairs in his day and owned slaves. The slave quarters still stood there. But things were on the decline. Nobody ever accused Bill Melvin of overwork. If he was out behind the barn with the strawstack to shield him and if the cork was out of the bottle, he might venture to sample the contents. Bill was a good man in many ways, he was honorable, but he wasn't a Christian.

Bill, I guess, was very smart. He fixed up all sorts of little machines at the mill. Besides the corn burr, he had a lathe and turned out chairs and things. He rigged up a hominy beater that would beat the hominy, break up the corn, sieve it, and make the finest hominy you ever ate. Those machines were his shrine. He never made any money at them. The time he spent waiting for somebody to bring in a little corn or something far exceeded the toll he collected.

Bill never had a large circle of friends. But on rainy days and snowy days Jake Crumley would come down to Bill's shop. It didn't have a chimley nor a stove, but they'd take shavings and sticks and build a little open campfire on a wrought iron disk there in the middle of the dirt floor. They'd sit and talk. One or the other would go home with the other for dinner. Then they'd go back and sit out the rest of the day. In that kind of a fashion they spent their years.

Old Squire Jim Melvin had the misfortune to lose a horse. They hooked the other horses to it and pulled it far out into the farm. Buzzards was soon swarming around the carcass, and somebody discovered that one of the buzzards had a bell on. The word got around, and the young men of the country would sneak up, wait till the buzzards collected, and then flush them out to hear the bell ring. Nobody ever knew how that buzzard got belled or where he went to after the horse was gone. But that buzzard was the talk of the countryside for a while. I've read and preserved a few clippings about belled buzzards. One in Grainger County a few years back may have been the same buzzard as ours.

On Knob Creek there was an unusual number of mills and shops and crafts places. Among them was George Miller. He was a great manufacturer. He owned a shop, he owned a mill, he owned a saw mill. And besides owning mills he manufactured mills. George Miller owned five water wheels, turned by the waters of Knob Creek within a given distance of about three miles. First he had a water wheel in the forebay right at his house, that turned the grindstone, the churn, and a brood of other little machines about his home. Next was the big overshot wheel for his two-story shop, his factory where he manufactured saw mills, thrashing machines, horse powers, cutting boxes, and sundry other gadgets for the farm. Third was the wheel for his saw mill and another one for grinding meal in the same building. Fifthly, and on down stream half a mile, was the large overshot wheel for George Miller's three-story flour mill. Five wheels he had.

I well remember the old man. George was not too polished. He was in the rough. But he was the best mechanic that ever was hatched in all that whole country. George Miller invented and manufactured a thrashing machine known as the Groundhog Thrasher, which wâs sold all over the country before the more modern thrashing machines got on the market. I know where there is one still intact, sitting in an old barn, just perfect for a museum.

In 1892-3, when the World's Fair was held in Chicago to commemorate the discovery of America in 1492, George Miller's sons attended that fair. A man by the name of Ferris had invented the Ferris wheel, and the first Ferris wheel ever operated in America was operated at the 1892-93 Chicago World's Fair. The boys stood by, looked it over, brought the idea back, and manufactured a Ferris wheel in George Miller's shop.

Judge Patterson was a well-to-do gentleman, a man of affairs in his day. But he lost his hearing and, of course, was not suitable as a judge of the court any longer. He lived in a mile of George Miller, and he heard it talked about, about George a-building a Ferris wheel. He rode horseback down to see the sight. The judge had a rather peculiar way of getting the conversation understood between him and somebody else. He says, "Well, George, I understand you're building a Ferris wheel. If you are, nod your head, and if you aren't, shake it." George nodded his head. "Well, I came down to see what it looks like." George motioned him to come around and look it over. The judge looked it up and down and all around and says, "Well, George, I'm proud to see the thing built. I think purty soon everybody on Knob Creek will be like to have one."

As a little boy I remember seeing the George Miller Ferris wheel. His sons operated it on big days, Fourth of Julys, during the fair, and at show days in Johnson City. First they ran it with horsepower, and later with a stationary engine. Folks traveled for miles to see the thing even if they didn't ride it. Everybody wondered how in the world can you stay on when it goes over. If a boy had a quarter, he and his girl could ride the George Miller Ferris wheel. It wasn't such a big one, but they had sure been somewhere and had a unique experience. But you know, that thing got destroyed. If we had it now, what a marvelous relic it would be.

My Great Uncle Dan'l Bowman was the possessor of a written legend that's been handed down about a mystery silver mine, long abandoned. The mine was described as being at a spot where "the river could be seen in three directions." The name of the river was not given, but the silver there was so plentiful that the finder could outfit his horses with silver shoes. A big-size stone laid over the hole where they could enter and go down and find the silver. Great Uncle Dan'l spent a lifetime hunting the spot. They'd ride far up into the mountainous headwaters of the Nolichucky, the Watauga, and the Holston. They would camp and search and look. He was a geologist and brought back hundreds of rare stones. But he never found a spot where a river could be seen in three directions.

Great Uncle Dan'l was a deacon in the Knob Creek church. When I was about four years old, he was sitting on the deacons' bench and somebody was a-preaching. He slumped forward and groaned out. One of the sisters just across the aisle said, "See what's the matter with Uncle Dan'l." Right out loud in church she said it. They shook him but he wouldn't wake up. They stretched him out dead. Great Uncle Dan'l died firmly believing the legend. A son of his searched a lifetime, first with his father, then with his own son, and that grandson, Will Bowman, is sure the mine is there waiting for to be discovered. I rather suspect myself that this silver mine is a reality if we could only find it.

When Reuben Sellers, who plowed on Sunday, died a natural death and his wife did too and his children were grown and gone, the farm was bought by Bill and Clemmy Vaughn. A tip of their farm cornered with my father's farm. The Vaughns were good people in their own way, happy-go-lucky, good neighbors and good livers. They were all great people to eat. They put up more corn and turnips and cabbage and punkins and pork and beef and canned fruit and dried fruit than anybody in the country. People said, the Vaughns were rich and didn't know it.

The two hundred acre Vaughn farm had a mile of creek bottom, the most of any farm around, and that bottom produced hay and corn in abundance. Mr. Vaughn was a stonecutter by trade; he didn't know how to farm. They didn't weed their corn much but always had a fair crop. Bill Vaughn was a great lover of horses; he had horses for every purpose and a number he never used at all. Colts would be born out in a field and sometimes die out there because none of the Vaughns noticed. They'd have forty or fifty head of cattle, and they'd build stacks of hay in the meadows and fence them with rails. If the cows broke down the rails and tromped down the whole stack, that didn't excite anybody on the Vaughn farm. To give you an idea of how wealthy they were, they littered the horses' stables with hay. If a few hogs got in a corn field or slept in the crib, Bill Vaughn paid no attention to that.

They had large turnip patches and raised cabbage by the hundreds of heads. They'd bury the cabbage, bury the turnips, bury the apples, bury the potatoes to live on during the winter. The corn fields, particularly in the rich creek bottom, yielded multitudes of punkins. It'd take several men with a wagon two or three days to haul them in. Mr. Vaughn would put a man in the middle of his long garden plowing and throwing the dirt out and a couple of men shoveling it out. Then he'd take those wagonloads of punkins and build them up pyramidical in a long row that would be eight foot through at the bottom and two or three hundred feet long. They'd bring in the fodder and shock it over the punkins, and the men would shovel the dirt back against the stubble of the fodder.

Later Bill Vaughn would begin feeding the fodder, broach the punkin hoard, and have succulent feed for cattle, hogs, horses, and Vaughns. Aunt Clemmie was an old-time cook. They had punkin pie all the time. And early in the morning she'd put on a big pot of turnips. She'd go to their barrelful of salted-down hog jowls with the teeth still in and fetch one to season the turnips. That'd be their main dish, along with big dodgers of corn bread, baked in a baker on the fireside, and good strong coffee. If they had any dessert besides punkin pie, it was dried apples, stewed dried fruit, or dried peach pie. The next day the menu would be hog jowl and cabbage, and the next, a peck of Irish potatoes and a big ham bone. It was rough food for rough people; but in their own style the Vaughns provided themselves with a healthy, balanced ration.

Bill Vaughn had the best watermelon patch in all that country. In it he erected an ash hopper and filled it with horse manure. He watered the melon hills with the black ooze that filtered through. He had huge prize melons for market, and many folks caught up on visiting the Vaughns right during watermelon season. The Vaughns had so much food that neighbors were all the time coming in to help them eat it.

Aunt Clemmie was a great hand to visit, herself, and she knew how to get a visit in. She'd hint around to my mother till she'd get invited over. Then she'd casually say, "Becky, you do have the best fried chicken I ever did eat.'' Mother used to say, ''A short horse is soon curried''—a modest meal is quickly prepared—but it couldn't be quite that way for Aunt Clemmie.

She'd come. Mother'd call dinner. We children'd be on the bench, Father at the head of the table, and Mother at the foot of the table on the opposite side where she could pour coffee or milk or whatever. Aunt Clemmie'd be between Mother and Father. She loved to talk. Pappy'd be waiting on the table and edge in: ''Yer choice of chicken?''

''Alfred, I want the straw bonnet,'' she'd say. That's the piece that has the ribs and part of the neck and very little meat; she called it the straw bonnet. John and I, we just kinked over. She invariably asked for the boniest piece.

Bill Vaughn and Clemmie Carr Vaughn were divorced twice and ended up marrying each other three times. But early one morning he headed for the barn to feed, while Aunt Clemmie prepared breakfast. Bill Vaughn was never seen by his family again. He took with him only the two effects he treasured most: a fine silver watch and his Winchester rifle. There come rumors every once in a while, even one that he was on the isle of Jamaica cutting stone for the government. But every time his son Sam made a trip to follow up a rumor, it was all a cold trail.

The Vaughns are all dead now and the farm is nearly gone. What was a cow path is now a highway; what was a rabbit patch is an open air drive-in theater. Where cattle and horses grazed is business property and places of amusement. The rich creek bottom is cut into subdivisions and lots for Johnson City as it bulges out and out.

Chapter Seven

"DOWN ON THE CARPET YOU MUST KNEEL"

A little boy and girl out of different families get together quick and play with dolls, shoot marbles, and bat balls; they are congenial one with the other. But as the child grows and sex develops, timidity comes, which is the God-given counterpart to protect him from going overboard on sex. Timidity and bashfulness may follow through a period from, say, eight years old to fifteen or more. Then it begins to wear out. It ought to fade sometime, because you oughtn't to be bashful when you're twenty. If timidity held on till you was forty, you'd never mate, and I've seen a few cases where it apparently did.

When I was about fifteen, there was a girl'd come to our place; she'd walk in the front door, and I'd run out the back. And if I went over on her place, she hid. I'd be setting at the table and glance up quick: she'd be peeping around the corner at me and dodge back. We never had any case of any kind; I was just looking her over, and she was looking me over. (She's dead now; she married somebody else and had a big family.)

As timidity wears out, judgment comes along, judgment that tells a girl not to break over and a boy to keep himself in check. But you can break timidity down in tender years, and sex will run riot. And that's what we're doing in the schools. The moral situation in the country is shot.

My father and my mother protected me; I never ran headlong into immoral situations. They steered me away from poke suppers and wild games and dances. But I went to butter boilings and gatherings of various kinds. Couples'd form, there'd be things to eat. A boy'd take his girl and go out and sit down on a bench or chairs or on the ground. They'd have a good time and talk and feed each other out of one another's spoon. Then that'd get a little bit old and break up, and he'd find another girl and some more refreshments.

About the only kissing game I ever remember participating in went like this. You have a circle and one person in the middle by himself. The crowd circles around singing,

"Go forth to face your lover;
I measure my love to show you,

O Willy, how I love you!
O Willy, how I love you!
Down on this carpet you must kneel,
Kiss your true love in the field."

If I was the boy in the middle, I'd just walk over to my favorite girl. Everybody stops but sings right on. When they come to "Down on this carpet," she kneels and I kneel, and at the painful command "Kiss," we do. Was that too loud?

My timidity slackened up some. Going to school and walking home, we'd fall in company with the girls. Handy it was to straggle along with Lonie Brown. I walked her backwards and forwards, from school and to school. We got to be quite familiar. I proposed to her—joking. She'd grab my arm and say, "Yes, indeed; that'll be wonderful." It was a joke with me and with her too, I guess; but she was responding purty good.

In the Knob Creek church there were, I suppose, thirty-five or forty young people, and nearly every one of them was a cousin to me. If they weren't a first cousin, they were a second or a third. We were thrown together a great deal, all in the same circle, and didn't have many outside friends. I was taught against first cousins and second cousins; it oughta be third, and that'd be a little dangerous. But if you got overwhelmed and off of your balance, a marriage might shape up regardless. Being with my cousins all the time, that came purty near happening to me. But a first cousin just wouldn't do, and I never got carried away with a third cousin.

Another considerable problem was what work I would do in life. I thought a good deal about medicine. Dr. Fox was a real old-time doctor. What he knew about anatomy and the sick body he got from practicing and not out of books. He was a purty well-informed old man. One day he came to my father's house to see my mother; she was sick. It was not, though, a case of confinement or childbirth. He wore his hat in the house and kept it crushed down odd-shaped. When through with examining Mother, he walked his chair clear up to the fireplace and got to talking to Daddy. He chewed tobacco and every little while he'd spew a big one into the fire. There had been a spot close to the moon, observed by the astronomers, and that was in the papers. Dr. Fox, he was purty excitable about anything that was new, and he'd splutter: "That spot up there means somethin', Alferd." You'd've thought a monster was swallering the moon to hear Dr. Fox talk.

Well, I spoke to Dr. Fox about my interest in medicine, and Mother and Daddy did too. In those days you went and read under a doctor. You could read under a doctor two or three years, then do a little post-graduate work, get an examination, and start practicing yourself on people. I decided to undertake it. I rode over to Dr. Fox's house horseback. He picked from his shelves the books he thought would be good for me to master. They were each thick as a fence rail. One of them was Pancourts Wooster—maybe that was the author. Riding home, I got caught in a downpour without any wrops, so I turned off of the road into a barn-shed, dismounted, tied up my horse, and read the first chapter in Pancourts Wooster as the rain beat down.

I brought that book and the others on home. I'd look at it, read patches from it, think and dream over it. But I never made much headway in it.

My father was a Christian, but he was a good politician. He was elected road commissioner and school commissioner. He enumerated the children, and he enumerated the census. Father stood well in politics, for which he didn't see any harm. Walter Preston Brownlow was the congressman, had been for a number of years, and stayed in office a long time. He had a strong organization, of which Father was a member. He kept his eye always open for anything he could do for his constituents, and my father was a constituent.

Walter Preston Brownlow took a list of young men over the country in families that was his supporters, and I got on the list. He sent the list to West Point. I didn't solicit nor even know about it. Father didn't neither, I'm sure. Daddy and Mother were, of course, adverse to war and my going to West Point. But I began to receive fat envelopes, and over in the corner was always these words: MEN-O-WAR. I read all those letters with their stories about glory, education, seeing the world, and they purty near knocked my persimmon. I could see my convictions hanging fire between two contrary opinions. But I steered by, and got by somehow, and never went to West Point.

About 1906 a vacancy occurred in the mail route at Johnson City. John Campbell, the postmaster, was a very good friend of my father. He and Congressman Walter Preston Brownlow thought Reuel ought to take the examination; he'd be in good line to have the position. It would be a Civil Service examination, but strings could be pulled, and they'd pull them for me. When we met in the Science Hill School building in Johnson City, there was thirty-two men took that test for the one position. I thought I did purty well in it, but I didn't hear a thing for more than a year. I worked on the farm, I helped build a railroad; I waited and listened, but no word came. John Campbell didn't give us any satisfaction, nor nobody knew a thing about it.

The first Saturday in August, 1908, the old Knob Creek church held an election for ministers. I happened to be elected. The impact of that on me was profound; I was swept off of my feet. As far back as I can remember I had the inkling or call to be a Dunker preacher; I was born with it. And the election confirmed and certified and climaxed the call.

School at Daleville College in Virginia was beginning the first of September. I had less than a month to decide what to do. I threw down everything and got ready to go to school at Daleville and prepare for the Brethren ministry. After I was already at Daleville a month, an official-looking letter came: I'd got that position as mail carrier. But I had by then firmly decided on the ministry and was away in college preparing for it; so I turned the job down and left it for somebody else.

I had, though, run a great risk: if that commission had arrived any time before August or before that election, I would no doubt have accepted the $1200 salary and carried letters. I'd have worn out several nags and a Ford car or two. And if I'd've survived through it, I'd now be settled down in Washington County as an old retired worn-out mail carrier.

But my election to the Christian ministry changed everything: it took me away from that mail carrier's job, which would have been a damnable setup, and it snatched me away from my cousins and my local social possibilities.

Chapter Eight

THE SANDY-COLORED BEARD

I never got really tangled up in a love affair until I went to college. We hadn't much more than arrived at Daleville when they stretched a curtain across the auditorium and herded the girls all onto the stage end and us boys over on the other side. The curtain of mystery between went clear across, dragging the floor, and was up within two feet of the ceiling. Each girl made a heart out of colored paper, inscribed her name under the front fold, put her heart on a fishhook, and slung it across the curtain to us on a line. We boys would surge toward each new bait that come dangling down. No telling who you might get hooked by, and the girl couldn't know who she was gonna ketch. And you couldn't be too careless grabbing, or you'd stick a hook in your hand.

I kept jumping and grabbing toward every heart and finally pinched holt of one. The heart was Miss Noffsinger's. She caught me, and I went along with her. She was a good-looking portly kind of a girl, black-headed and black-eyed. We sat together in the auditorium, discussed different matters, got well acquainted, and so forth. When everybody had caught somebody, the curtain was pulled down, and we had the whole auditorium for social games. At each tap of a bell everybody changed partners. I did my best to keep up with the crowd. Miss Noffsinger, though, was the only one that commanded my best attention. (I have that pink paper heart yet.)

Well, I began keeping company some with Miss Noffsinger. But toward Christmas I noticed that about every other Friday there'd be a fine new rubber-tired buggy with a black horse in patent-leather harness drive up to Central Hall. A young man would escort Miss Noffsinger out to the buggy, help her in, crack the buggy whip, and drive away with her at a lope. I was hoping it was her brother. But upon making inquiry I found out it was her best boy from her home neighborhood, not more than forty miles distant. I didn't stand a ghost of a show. She was a-making a dishrag out of me and a tablecloth out of him. Totally without a marriage ceremony, I changed her name a little and would tell the boys, "Miss Nuff-said is gone."

There was in the main hall of the college a winding, pleasantly narrow staircase. The bell would ring, and the class from one of the recitation rooms upstairs would come pouring down, and we in the next class would be pushing our way up. We'd meet and get all conglomerated. I've seen some high-handed fun and even some kissing there on that winding stair.

There wasn't so many of us at Daleville that wore the Brethren plain clothes. I did. With most of the girls, though, there was a little slant of plainness that would distinguish them from Hollins Institute, the girls' college right next to us. I never did go over there a-courting, but many of our boys did sometimes.

What with a winding staircase and other arrangements, I got acquainted with a girl from Franklin County, Virginia, by the name of Bessie Barnhart and was trying to switch over to her. It was easier for me with Bessie than it was with Miss Noffsinger; I began giving her my best attention and we became purty tolerable good friends.

I hadn't, though, been in college over two weeks when misfortune struck me low. Daleville church was right up from the college a ways. Wilbur Peters roomed straight across the hall from me. When he went to put his coat on, ready to go to church Sunday morning, a thread had broken and his sleeve ripped six inches under the arm. Wilbur was lamenting about it; his heart was set on wearing his best suit, but here the coat was, torn.

I says to him, "Let me fix that."

"Ah, ye can't fix it, can ye?"

"Yes," I says, "I believe I can."

Mother had provided me with a box of needles, thread, thimble, buttons, scissors, and everything—a nice selection. I studied the rip carefully and determined that the thread had broken and just come out; the goods was not broken at all. So I got inside and threaded through the same holes exactly, from where the rip started to where it came to an end. I took my finished product over and showed it to Wilbur. Of course he raised up the sleeve the first thing, and you couldn't even see the thread. He says to me, "Ye're a regular old mother."

The saying spread, and they called me "Mother Pritchett" as long as I went to college. I never got over that: "Mother Pritchett" or "Mother" it was for everything.

We had a girl by the name of Ruth Burger. She was on the third floor of the Central Hall, and I was on the second floor of the Denton Hall. Our buildings were close enough together until the shadder of one would go over against the other of an evening, a purty nice distance.

Ruth Burger had a Big Ben clock, a little round clock. It was a tricky timepiece. When it wouldn't run, she'd jiggle it, turn it upside down, joggle it some more. One day she just raised the window and slung old Big Ben out like a discus. She hurled it her best and it came angling clear across the campus from her building over to ours. It landed on the sidewalk, bounced, and tumbled further. I happened to be a-coming along just after the heave, so I picked up the clock a-laying there. It'd hit the sidewalk on one of the legs and drove the leg plumb up in it.

We had a watch tinker on our hall. I took Big Ben up to him and says, "George, I declare my clock needs oilin' or adjustin' someway. It won't run. I wish you'd see what's a matter with it."

"All right, Mother, I'll check it over." I handed the thing to him and went back to my room. I knew of course that he had something he couldn't do anything with, having a leg drove plumb up in it.

In a day or two he walked into my room and handed me Big Ben. It was just a-ticking to beat the band. I perched it on my study table and used it for years after that.

I would say I enjoyed college as much as any other person that ever went to college. I never missed a note any time. We had social nights and nights off; and especially on those occasions there was lots of maybe what you'd consider mischief. But I don't recollect anything I regret very greatly.

We had at Daleville a circle of boys known as the Buttermilk Gang. They'd visit springhouses or sometimes they'd sneak to some chicken roost, pull off a hen, roast her in the night, and have a feast. With honesty I can affirm that I never did belong to the Buttermilk Gang. But I have received some of the proceeds from their efforts.

Miss Bessie Barnhart's father was the longest-bearded man I'd ever heard of; his beard came down below hip level. A fellow named Johnson was always a-joking me about Old Man Barnhart's beard. When he found out I was heading over there to a Love Feast, he says, "Mother, you get a lock of the old man's beard. I warn you, if you really want to stand in with them, you'll need to get a lock of that beard."

I'd never met Brother Barnhart, but over at the church when I spotted this man with the longest flowing sandy beard I'd ever witnessed, I knew it must be him. And we met. I was at the Love Feast and read the thirteenth chapter of John for them at the feet-washing. I went over to the Barnharts to spend the night. There was a houseful of company, and Sister Barnhart set out a late lunch for us. I'd purty well met the young folks but not some old women and men. When they called us to the table I was being introduced around and was trying to be as courteous as I knew how. But, after all the introductions, here at the head of the table still stood a brother with a short beard. I went around and shook hands with him—and was I embarrassed: it was Brother Barnhart! He had buttoned up his beard under his Brethren vest and coat, so all he had showing was a little short beard. Wasn't that a snap for me to get in?

The next morning I strolled out to the Barnharts' barn and looked the cattle over. A way dawned on me to answer Johnson's challenge back at college. The beard in question was sandy—sandy color. I studied the shades of the cows' tails, snuck up on a perfect old Bossie, caught a-holt of her tail, and whacked out a piece. The wisp was longer than my hand and sandy. I tucked it away, carried it along back to Daleville with me, and suspended it in front of Johnson: "Here's Old Man Barnhart's beard."

"Darned if it ain't!" he exclaimed. I made a believer out of him.

Will the Lord forgive a man for doing such as that? Surely, good Lord, you wouldn't hold that against a boy.

The Brethren Annual Conference for 1909 was held at Harrisonburg, Virginia. The Norfolk & Western Railroad made up a special train. They got one carload at Christiansburg, a carload at Rocky Mount, two in Roanoke, a carload at Cloverdale. There was a hundred and one of us from Daleville College and community that got on at Cloverdale. Miss Bessie Barnhart had left college a day early to go home and get ready for the conference. I had engaged her company to and during the conference, and she was to be in the car from Rocky Mount. I entered the coach, rubbernecked around. She was at the end seat, sitting on half of the seat and her baggage was on the other half; she was saving me some room. I shook hands, put her grip and mine up overhead, sat down beside her, and had a chat for forty or fifty miles.

It was a hundred twenty-five miles or thereabouts to Harrisonburg. We was a-running purty good speed, but it'd take a couple hours to make it. I got up and sauntered down through the coach. I knew a lot of people, had been to a lot of churches, met a lot of young folks and older folks too. I was shaking hands and having a splendid time with the boys and the girls and the people I knew. I had no sooner got on up and entered the Christiansburg coach when I spotted a black-eyed, black-headed, well-built, wonderful-looking girl a-setting there. It flashed through me like lightning. I walked on to the end of the coach and slipped right in by the side of an old brother. I haven't got beard enough to make him a mustache. I whispered to him, "Say, uncle, who's the girl back there two seats from the back?"

He craned his neck around and croaked, "Which one?"

I was embarrassed but said softly, "The one on that second seat on the right from the back."

"Ella Poff," he bawled out.

"Where does she live?" I asked.

"She lives at Christiansburg."

I took a little daybook out of my pocket and jotted down: "Ella Poff, Chbg, Va." I returned it to my pocket, went on out and up through another coach and another. I mustered up enough of courage to head on back. When I stepped into the Christiansburg car, I was facing her, I could see her right in the face. It was a long railroad coach. I walked slow and generous and kept my eye on her till I got by. I saw her looking at me.

I strolled on back to the seat beside Miss Barnhart and we went on talking. I was engaged to be with her during the conference, and I stayed with my contract. But I saw Miss Ella on the grounds several times and I looked her over every chance I could, though I had no introduction to her.

In college that fall I got mighty well acquainted with Oliver Reed, a jovial young minister from Floyd County, Virginia. Along in November we were looking ahead, as college boys do, to Christmas times. I says to him, "Oliver, what you gonna do for Christmas?"

He says, "I'll go home, I guess. What're you gonna do?"

"I don't know, Oliver. It's a long ways back to my home, a hundred sixty miles, and I don't have extra money to throw away."

A day or two later he says, "You just go home with me."

I pondered on it a bit and graciously told him I thought maybe I could. We got to discussing how the evening train went just to Christiansburg, and he lived thirty miles further over. I didn't have any hotel money, so I says, "What would you do that night?"

He says, "I've got a girl up there."

"That's interesting," says I. "What's her name?"

"Miss Poff," he said.

I fell flat as a flitter. I knowed it was Ella he was a-talking about. I was fingering my little daybook with "Ella Poff, Chbg, Va." and asked casual, "What kin is your girl to Ella Poff?"

"Ella Poff? What do you know about Ella Poff?"

That scared me worse. I says, "I asked you what kin your girl was to her."

"They're sisters—Berthie and Ella. How'd you know Ella?"

My spirits was soaring, and I says, "Did Miss Ella go to the Annual Conference last year?"

"Yes, she was in that Christiansburg car."

I told him, "I saw Ella Poff on that train. I didn't have any acquaintance with her, but I saw her on that train. When you write your girl, Berthie, you tell her there was a boy on that train says, tell her sister Ella hello." Oliver put that in his letter. In a week or so he heard back and the sister Berthie gave some little, very limited amount of information for me.

At Christmas, Oliver and I headed for Christiansburg on the evening train. The Poff family sent over to the depot after us. They had a big old-time Virginia Brethren chicken supper. Two rooms of theirs they used for parlors. The four of us, Oliver and Berthie, Ella and me, were in the one parlor. But Oliver knew his girl real well, he wanted to be by themselves, so they retired to the other room. I was proud of him for it; that suited me fine, and Ella suited me wonderful. We got along splendid in the conversation that night. At the end of the holidays we made it back only as far as Christiansburg and needed to stay all night again at the Poffs. I screwed up enough of courage to ask Ella for a correspondence and she accepted.

During the next few months I had to go up to East Radford and thereabouts several times to preach, and it was handy to stop by the Poffs. The coals of fire were glowing. But the following summer I was back among the mountain churches preaching, had a different post office every few days, and lost out on my correspondence entirely. Close to the first of September there was a Sunday school reunion near Christiansburg, and of course I couldn't miss it. I just accidentally stopped around to see Miss Ella, expecting to take a whipping. But we fixed things up in good style.

Things were approaching the point that even though I wasn't engaged I said to Oliver, who was, "Let's get married the same day and at the same time, if I can get along as well as you have. The way we'll do it, we'll stand opposite each other; I'll say your ceremony, and after I get yours said, you'll say mine. We'll have a double wedding out of it, Oliver." That just suited him acceptable. Of course I was on a broken shoestring because I had no engagement, and we'd had that falling-apart in the summertime.

But later in the fall his girl Berthie got appendicitis and it developed into peritonitis, which poisoned her all over. She died. But Ella lived, and on September 29, 1911, we were married. We got on a train at Christiansburg, and that night in a Bristol hotel we had our first family altar.

Chapter Nine

THE TREMBLE OF THE TRAIN

Attending Daleville College did a number of things for me: I got prepared for the ministry in a limited way at least; I met the girl who became mother of my family; I was preserved from living out my days as a local mail carrier; and I've spent well over half a century traveling all over the country in missions of the church, with the joy of going to conferences, holding revivals, preaching the Gospel, baptizing applicants, solemnizing marriages. It's been a great life.

It was December 2, 1908, at the Boones Creek church in Tennessee that I preached my first sermon. Brother A. M. Laughren was holding a revival. He got bronchitis, and his voice was so shot by the one service that he asked me to preach for him the next night and give his throat a rest. I told him I would. I never had preached yet.

Night came and I was a little weak-kneed. Brother Laughren was present on the platform with me, and so was Uncle Joe Bowman, an old experienced elder. While they were singing the last song, I whispered over to Uncle Joe, "Won't you preach for Brother Laughren tonight, Uncle Joe?"

"No—no, go ahead. Say whatever ye wanta say, and I'll lay up the gaps fer ye." He meant he'd patch up my mistakes. Wasn't that encouragement for a boy? He knew I'd throw them down. So I stood up on my weak knees and preached. My text was, "He that gathereth not with me scattereth abroad." I put in twenty-five or thirty minutes and at the end of everything closed the service—before an audience that was expecting Laughren to preach. Of course we had to assure the folks that Brother Laughren would be back the next night or there'd have been an empty house.

When I was young and in my prime, I was purty energetic and daring, I guess. When we'd be together in a crowd, I worked at the head of the column. I planned the tasks, clumb the ladders, waded the river, or whatever was to do. I didn't mind going ahead; I was expected to do that, and I willingly did it.

I was at Knob Creek after they tore down the old log church (which I tried to keep them from doing) and built the new church. I was sitting up on the platform at the preachers' bench, which ran lengthways of the building, along with the other ministers. Facing the brother who was preaching, I could also look out over the hitch lot. There wasn't an automobile on the grounds, but everywhere were the horses for the buggies, hacks, and horseback riders. I got distracted from the sermon when I saw a horse break loose from his station and go pushing along next to a horizontal hitching pole, unloosing several other horses, and him still hitched to his buggy.

It was summertime. The window was up. I sprung to that windowsill, turned a flip out of the church while the man was a-preaching, lit eight foot on down. I dashed over, caught the horse and saved any kind of further trouble. It was done so fast a number of people didn't see what happened or what became of me. They only saw something dark splash out through the window.

During my life I never had a salary in the ministry. Ella and I, we ate with the chickens for a few years. When I moved down to pastor the French Broad church, I canvassed the forty members—wife and I made forty-two—and they subscribed a total of $45 for the first year as the church budget. Generous though they are, I never knew them later to take up an offering for the preacher and sit at my mailbox waiting to give it to me. And for the denomination too I've done many a thank-you job.

I left Daleville with a college debt. Ella and I were just married and wanted to set up housekeeping. I snatched up an awful good job at a farmers' store in Johnson City, which paid the high wage of 90¢ a day. They didn't need me but two or three days out of the week. I was already into the ministry head and ears, pastoring churches on Sunday; but the rest of my time I put in raising some crops on a little farm I had bought. The store business grew, they needed me every day, and paid me $1 a day. The business kept growing and they paid me $1.25, $1.50, $2 a day. I finished off paying for the farm and raised a few crops too. Our four children, Gomer, Ethel, Erlene, and Evelyn, were all born there on that place.

I quit working for the store about 1918 when I had thirteen weeks of typhoid fever. I was five weeks delirious. Four Brethren elders came to anoint me. My earthly life was very nearly cut off then. My hair shed out by handfuls, and my whiskers, my eyebrows and eyelashes. All of my hair all over came out. My head was as bald as a teacup and slick as my watch. But I survived. My hair and beard finally began to grow back in. I laid away my white-handled Tonsorial Gem razor and never shaved again. I still have that razor, though some of my womenfolks pulled a tack with it and broke a gap in it as big as a wheat grain and ruined the razor; but I still have it.

I was so glad to get my hair back and my beard back, and I just let her grow. It wasn't that I had to wear a beard to be religious; I wasn't ever that cranky, though there was still then yet a considerable amount of preaching exhorting brethren to wear the beard. With me it was grateful appreciation for having my hair back again. My hair, by the way, was very curly. It wasn't black and it wasn't red; it was auburn. My beard was a little darker.

Galen Royer, when he was a young man, he wore a full beard. He was about my age. At the Annual Conference, after he had shaved and I had started a beard, I shook hands with him and he says, "I can't place ye."

I says, "I put on what you took off."

"Oh," he laughed, "it's Pritchett."

Well, when any centennial comes along, I'm already ready. My beard has led me into many experiences. I was in an elevator one time, and a boy six or eight years old shouted, "Take that off of there," and he jumped up and grabbed my beard. He thought it was a false beard. He'd probably never seen a man with a beard, but only Santa Claus.

After you're well-known with a beard, there's no way back. I'm recognized everywhere now in all kinds of crowds and gatherings. If I was to shave, I'd be ruined. If I was to take off my beard and go to Annual Conference with a lapel coat and a big cravat, nobody'd know me.

I've been preaching already in a couple of churches when they caught afire. But with neither of them was it final; they didn't burn up. I was preaching at the Beaver Creek church in Tennessee when a neighbor's house got afire, and my audience all run out on me to help carry the goods out of the home that was a-burning. The Pleasant View church in Washington County had a masterful big desk made out of inch-and-a-half walnut. One winter night we were commenting about what a marvelous piece of walnut this was. The desk wasn't artistic or nicely made, but it sure did have the material. I stayed in the community that night, and the church burnt down, with nobody there, and all that walnut went up in flames.

Down in Nocona, Texas, if they hear it thunder, you don't have to say, "Meeting dismissed." You ain't got time; they run for the storm cellars. I was preaching there once, and almost before I knew it the benches were all empty. The storm wasn't too severe, but they wouldn't take no risk. A twister in that country can almost plow the ground where it passes through.

Hornets already have driven me out of the pulpit. I was down at the Bakers Cross Roads church to preach, and a bunch of hornets had a nest in a tree just outside a window which we had down to ventilate. The hornets were attracted by the light and swarmed into the house. We had to raise that transom and go to eliminating hornets before we could go ahead with the meeting that night.

I've been in church various times when somebody had a fainty spell or a real fit. Once while I was preaching down in the Beaver Creek church, an old sister had one of her frequent fits. She reached up, grabbed holt of the two strings of beads around her neck, jerked them asunder, and slung the beads, raining them all over the house. A time or so somebody's fell over and died, listening to me preach.

I really don't talk much. I don't talk except when I'm by myself or with somebody or when I want to talk. But wherever I go, at country stores, in barber shops, and particularly on trains, I seem to collect a crowd. There'll be conductors, college girls, tottery ladies, boy scouts. I lead the conversation, rehearse to them divers topics, but do not however preach. What with traveling around so much, I know people in wholesale more than in retail.

I never was a railroad man, but I've always been a railroad customer, having made hundreds and hundreds of trips by train in the work of the church. A railroad man has to get awfully old before he can retire and be entirely satisfied, because he wants to hear the rattle of the train. I'm the same way: I like to hear the rattle. I like to hear the car wheels grind the rails on a curve. The tremble of a train is soothing to me. I like to hear the whistle blow. I like to see the crowds get on and off and friends meet friends. I like to hear the conductor call out, "All aboard."

During the First World War, I made several trips on the long straight stretch in South Carolina between Spartansburg and Columbia. I was on good trains, and they didn't stop. But almost constantly all through that night's ride the train would blow: *Weeeoooh, weeooh, weooh-weooh-weooh*. I enquired into it and was told that the engineer on that track had run over a buggy with his girl in it, and the horse, buggy, and flesh of the girl was all mangled together. The engineer never married, never courted anybody else. It happened on this line; and when he left Spartansburg he kept the whistle open all the way. That's what I was told. I've ridden trains in every state of the Union except Maine and Montana, and in Canada, Mexico, and Europe, but that between Spartansburg and Columbia was the most weird, mournful train-blowing I ever heard in my life.

In the First World War, I had an assignment from the Brotherhood to visit the Army camps to correct any irregularities that might happen with boys not well-informed on the noncombatant principle or who were being forced into the Army to carry arms and wear uniforms when it was against their conscience. I made trips to camps all over the eastern half of the United States. Transportation was hard to obtain. Standing room was at a premium on most all common carriers. I've ridden dark, crowded coaches when the aisles were crammed with soldiers fast asleep. Many a night I've been glad to sleep in a rough attic of a hotel near a large soldier camp.

On one occasion I carried a treasonous letter to a boy that was a noncombatant in Camp Jackson, Columbia, South Carolina. His brother had been inducted into the Army, and when he went down the gangplank in France, he mailed a letter off to his brother's girl in Tennessee, and she was to attend to it that the brother got this personal message from him: "Don't go to the Army. Go to hell first." The girl and her mother came to me. They wasn't over-urgent about it but did hope I'd get the letter to him.

I traveled to Camp Jackson with that letter. But the boy was locked up behind barb-wire because he wouldn't obey their orders. He stood pat, so they threw him in the guardhouse, which was inside what they called the depot brigade, far on the inland of the camp, and the camp had forty thousand soldiers in it. No civilian could enter the depot brigade unless he had a pilot.

General French was the head man of all the camps in the United States, and his headquarters happened to be at Camp Jackson. I decided to pay him a visit because I wanted to get inside the depot brigade and carry the secret letter to this boy there in the guardhouse. General French, when I entered, he called a stenographer, and every word I said and every word he said was a matter of record. I got the general convinced. He says, "Mr. Pritchett, if you can be of any assistance, we'd be happy to have you. I'm gonna send you a pilot. You can't go in there by yourself." He rung a bell, a soldier came, and orders were given.

We walked and walked and walked and walked and finally got to the depot brigade. But then we needed to get permission from the local man that was in charge. I went in to present my case and obtain permission. When I got back to the door, my pilot was gone. The man he says to me, "How'd you get in here?"

I says, "I had a pilot."

"How'd you get a pilot?"

"I got a pilot from General French."

"Where is your pilot?" says he.

"I don't know."

He says, "I don't know that you had one. You're subject to arrest." He smote a bell, a couple of sergeants marched up, and I was under arrest. It was in the hot midsummertime. I was ordered inside of a barb-wire enclosure with the barb-wire thick right straight up twelve feet and on out the crossarms. They detailed a man to stand by me, to be my guard. There was a little pine tree inside, and I asked to stand in the shade of the tree. He denied me that privilege. So I stood in the broiling hot sun.

I was ruminating what I might contrive and how I might handle the letter which was in my coat pocket, that letter which said, "Don't go to the Army. Go to hell first." That was seditious, and I knew it—seditious for the writer and seditious for me. I had a little square collar box with a lunch in it. I unpacked my dinner, got several letters out of my pocket, and shuffled that one down under the paper that laid in the bottom of the collar box. I stuffed my lunch back in and ate some of it, of which he paid no attention to. But I'd stole a march on him right there.

I stood in the sun for four or five hours until the powers that be graciously granted me the chance to have a military trial. I was marched by two guards with rifles over and down and through and across till we finally arrived at the judge's office. Man after man was being tried, soldiers, civilians, all kinds. I was standing in line. My turn came, and I stepped into the circle in front of the judge. And the judge said to the guards, "What's your man done?"

"Sir," they charged, "he was spreading seditious literature in the depot brigade." They hadn't seen the letter, but I was carrying the President's Declaration on Noncombatants and some Brethren Conference statements. These they saw. A declaration from the President of the United States they regarded as seditious literature, but they hadn't got holt of the letter from the soldier in France which was really seditious.

The judge said, "What do you want to do with your man?"

"You're the one to say, judge."

I says, "Judge, can I speak?"

"Speak, sir," he said. Everything was very precise.

I says, "Judge, your honor, I represent a church. There's some men of my faith in the guardhouse. I'm not spreading any seditious literature. I have declarations from my church Conference and from the President of the United States about noncombatants, and I had a pilot assigned me by General French. But after escorting me into the depot brigade, he gave me the dodge, so I was caught without a pilot, which is against your rules; but he slipped away while I went in to see the local officer in charge for getting into the guardhouse."

The judge turned around to my guardians and asked, "What do you want to do with him?"

They said, "You're the judge, you say."

The judge said, "You're excused." And I walked out. And he allowed me to go over and see Claude Simmons. We were granted permission to walk out of that guardhouse. There was a barrack built high off of the ground at one side, and we went under there. I unpacked my lunch and showed him the letter mailed by his brother in France with the counsel: "Don't go to the Army. Go to hell first." After he read it, I tucked it back under the paper below my half-eaten dinner. Then in purty short order I got outside of the depot brigade, got outside of the camp, caught a train, and came home. Later I married the boy and the girl the letter was mailed to.

I think it is ridiculous to run out on the battlefield and shoot somebody you ain't mad at. But if somebody's climbing in at the window wanting to take my pocketbook, on the spur of the moment, in an unguarded moment, I don't know what I might do. I've been in courts in Virginia and North Carolina and Tennessee defending conscientious objectors before high tribunals. One of the old pet questions the judge would ask, "Well, Mr. Pritchett, what would you do if a man'd be breaking into your home and threatening the life of your wife?"

I says, "Judge, I don't know what I might do on an unguarded moment, but I want you to know that I have no plans against him now. I have no murder in my heart against him now."

I've had innumerable adventures in my travels and can only rehearse a few. During the winter of 1933 I purchased a ticket in East Radford, Virginia, to go to Kermit, West Virginia. Before I got to Williamson, the conductor told me I'd have to get off at Williamson. I informed him that I had a ticket to Kermit. He says, "We don't stop at Kermit. This is a fast through train, and we never make no exceptions."

I, though, had the advantage of the situation; I had a ticket I purchased for Kermit and paid for. As we rolled into Williamson, I just leaned back and went to sleep, a possum sleep, and stayed in the coach. After we were on our way again, the conductor walked through and here I was still on the train. I got up and challenged him. There wasn't much argument and not very much said. He pulled that long through Norfolk & Western train to a stop at Kermit and left me off.

Kermit is on the Tug Fork of the Sandy River, and I was on my way to the Wolf Creek Church of the Brethren, twelve miles on up Wolf Creek over on the Kaintucky side. But it was midnight and cold. There were no lights nor street lights in the entire town of Kermit, nobody to meet me, nowhere to go for the rest of the night. I didn't see a police nor nobody anywhere.

I was acquainted with John Henry Fields and his wife Alice. They were members of the Wolf Creek church and operated a small boardinghouse, sometimes referred to as a hotel, located on the way to the river bridge across the Sandy at the state line. I ventured toward that hotel. Darkness and quiet prevailed inside and outside the old structure. I knocked at the door gently. No answer. I knocked more energetically, but no response. Discovering that the door was not locked, I made an entry and stumbled around in the dark of the strange lobby. Uneasy I was lest I might be taken for a burglar or an intruder.

Footsteps came through a hall, a door opened, and there stood John Henry Fields in his night clothes. He immediately snapped on the light, recognized me, and said, "Lo, here's the preacher and not an empty bed in the house."

I assured him that was all right; I was happy to get in out of the cold and would gladly set by the stove till morning.

"Could ye rest on this settee better than on a chair?" he asked.

"Oh, yes," says I, inconsiderately, whereupon he fetched a pillow and cover and said, "The first man gits up in the morning I'll fix ye a bed."

Brother Fields retired, and I tried to. I examined the settee. It had a high headboard, a high footboard, and a wide backboard, all square and upright. The seat was all rounded up, convexed and full of stiff springs. I turned out the light and cramped myself in between the headboard and the footboard, which was considerably shorter than my five feet, eleven inches. I had to do a balancing act to keep from rolling off of the rounded bottom. But the most confounded puzzle was how to arrange that cover. If it was right down on me, two-thirds'd be off on the one side and drag the rest onto the floor. But if I draped it partly up over the high backboard, the cover was over me but not on me, and there was a lively ventilation from head to foot. I tried every combination, every conceivable posture, but all with no avail. I remained as sleepless as on the train from East Radford to Kermit.

In my meditation during the long watches of that night I recalled a scripture found in Isaiah 28:20, quote: "For the bed is shorter than that a man can stretch himself on it: and the covering narrower than that he can wrap himself in it." I came to understand as never before Isaiah's description of how unrestful and miserable is the lost condition of a man who has sinned away his opportunities.

Toward sunup Brother Fields called for me to come and fill a bed which had just been vacated: comforting words. I took an hour or so of sleep, had breakfast, and started with my grip the twelve miles up the Wolf Creek dirt road. On one of the nights up there I ventured to use as my text Isaiah 28:20. And I believe I've preached on it half a dozen times since then.

Chapter Ten

"IF WE CONFESS OUR SINS"

I've had a wonderful lot of marrying experiences. I've married them in buggies, I've married them in the open, I've married them on the quiet, I've married them in the middle of the highway, I've married them in the wee hours of the night. I've said a ceremony in every room and hall of the courthouse at Dandridge and in the lobby of the jail.

A long while ago, when we still lived at Knob Creek, my family and I, we were on our way to church, and just at the end of the lane we met a boy and a girl in a buggy. He explained that he was coming to our house.

"Well, what can I do for ye?" I asked.

"We wanta git married."

I asked to see his papers. He pulled them out; I examined them and says, "Why, you bought these papers in Carter County, and we're in Washington County. I can't marry you here. We'll have to cross the line." I ruminated a bit and says, "I'm preachin' at Knob Creek today. You just wheel around here, you and your wife-to-be come to church; I'll preach, and then we'll cross the county line and I'll say the ceremony for ye."

Well, it was four or five miles over to the line and slow travel by buggy. When we got in the neighborhood purty close, I yelled to a man, "Sir, where's the county line?"

He says, "Ye see that house up there?"

"Yes."

"The Carter County line goes right through that house."

We drove on up. A man was out in the yard and I says, "Where's the Carter County line?"

"Right here splitting through this house," he says.

"I've got a couple here that wants to git married, and if you don't mind, we'd sure be obliged if we could use the Carter County end of your house for the ceremony."

You could tell by looking that he was a rough old customer. But he says, "Git out and come in." His wife was very nice.

"Now where's Carter County?" I asked to make sure.

"On that side of the hall," says he.

We stepped over into Carter County. I got through the ceremony and prayer and announced, "Congratulations are in order."

And if that crusty codger didn't flip into high key and say to this lad that had just been married the minute before, "You godforsaken old henpecked husband you."

Another time I had a letter from a girl over in Connarock, Virginia, wanting me to come up and say the ceremony for them, which I was glad to do. It was after a big snow and bitter cold. The wedding was to be at 4 p.m. and then a supper. Four o'clock arrived, and in the wintertime that was purty near dark, and Mr. Rudolph and Miss Lewis hadn't got back yet from going after their license. I wasn't too concerned; they'd be a bit late; they were driving a car on the mountain roads.

We waited till 5 p.m., till 6, till 7, and still no bridal pair. The house was full of people and some of the best folks of the country was present. We went ahead with supper, at which they had everything from smoked elephant down to jellied chiggers; it was quite a feast. Ever once in a while we'd hear a car and somebody'd yell, "They're here now!" But it wouldn't be them.

Finally at about 9 in the night the groom returned and the bride. He motioned me over into a side room and said, "We had the awfullest time at all."

I says, "What on earth has been the matter?"

"We couldn't get our license. We had to go all the way to Tennessee to get the license." The law in Virginia had just been passed that you had to have a blood test.

"Well," I sighted, "I'm terribly sorry, but you can't git married in Virginia with a Tennessee license."

"We know that," he says. "We're already married."

"Well," says I, "just don't say a word about it. I'll handle matters."

We arranged the wedding march, called folks in, got everything in good shape in every way. I was the only one besides the couple that knew they'd already been married. The procession started and they came on out. I was light on my grammar and said the ceremony in the past tense—and nobody discovered it. The past tense wouldn't break any precedent or any law. And some people, it was twenty-five years before they ever knew.

During my early ministry there was still yet in various places over the country a considerable amount of disturbance at public worship. Exercising as a young preacher, I was confronted with a great deal of it. Folks have come and asked me to hold a revival and said they needed a preacher and a sheriff combined. I've had drunks vomit vehemently right in worship. I've had wild boys go whipping and driving a buggy roughly down a road crowded with church people, hub a worm fence, horses loping, rails scattering everywhere. When things got real rough, I always told 'em: "We have to have order. I don't let the devil run away with my program. Understand that now."

During a revival at the Peak Creek church in North Carolina there was much disturbance night after night. I admonished the ones that were disturbing and also exhorted my constituency to quiet the situation so we could carry on the service. After I had done that a few times, the ungodly boys that were doing most of the disturbing, they stayed outside and made commotions. It was in the cold wintertime. One boy cracked the door open a little and had his head in listening. A fellow behind him gave a shove, which slammed the door around and sent him stumbling across the threshold. I said to my deacons, I says, "Will you go outside and keep the peace?" Dead silence prevailed. I said to one man, "Will you close the door?" He obliged me that far.

Right straight back of the pulpit this church had a big bay window set at three angles. I proceeded with trying to preach, but I could see my audience watching the various windowsashes back of me. I whirled around quick: those same boys were standing in the windows, gesturing and whispering to my audience. I struck for the front door, calling out, "If you'll keep the peace inside, I'll keep it outside."

With me marching down the aisle, the boys knew something was up. But they couldn't know whether I'd swing around on the one side of the church or the other. The church was atop a little hill with a barb-wire fence on every side but one, and there were bushes all around. The boys misjudged, and I met them at the middle window on the fenceless side. They ran over the bushes like cattle, darted down the hill, and loped into the creek, me right at their heels.

I collared one of the boys as he jumped in. The other two got on through and up into the bushes on the other side. I marched the boy up into the light of the window, held him there, and asked, "Young man, what's your name?" He told me a name and begged manfully to be loosed. I says, "I want to say to you that you're in serious trouble." I didn't promise him he'd get out of it lightly. I turned him loose, and he sneaked away.

A number of years ago in a revival at the Lone Star church in Tennessee, I had continuous disturbance night after night. It was an odd-built church with very poor oil lights and a dark corner where the boys would get with the girls, jerk their hair, and laugh out. I warned them, I had to get rough with them, I threatened prosecution. Finally I gave chase to one of them a hundred or two yards down the road. He got away, but that calmed things down for several nights.

Then another boy, a deacon's son, was over in the shadowy corner with a girl. He'd pinch her cheek, steal a kiss by hand, pull her hair. I called him on it a time or two, but whenever my eye was off of him, he'd be cutting up. I strode down out of the pulpit back into that corner, thrust my finger toward his face, and says, "Young man, if you don't behave yourself, I'm gonna throw you out." His features fell. It happened there was a committee assigning me around from place to place for dinner, and by Joe my place for dinner the next day was at that deacon's house and that same boy sat straight across the table from me.

At one meeting, as the summer pastor and I were walking to church, we found ourselves behind three men that were drinking, and one of them purty bad drunk. We were ketching up and the boys that weren't so drunk said to the other, "Come on. Don't ye see them d—n preachers follerin'?" We passed them, spoke to them, and moved on ahead. Weldon Flory, who was the janitor and the summer pastor, went on in to start the fire, light the old oil lamps, and do a lot of things. But I walked over to the nearest neighbor, who was chopping wood and says to him, "S'pose you come down to the church and help us keep the peace tonight?" I figured those drunks would show up.

"Oh, no," he crooned, "I wouldn't want to make anybody mad."

"Well, now, bless your life," says I. "We can't let the devil run away with our meeting, and we've had a lot of trouble already. I ask you as a citizen to come down and help us do something about it."

"They do that at the other churches."

"Well, I won't let 'em git away with it at mine."

We had the usual amount of song service and prayer. I took my text and was well started into my sermon, when those three drunks shuffled in. The fires had been so hot everybody moved back, and there was a long vacant bench right by the side of the glowing-hot stove. The trio took that bench. The drunkest boy soon stretched out, and the other two moved over and gave him room. Right in the middle of the sermon he rolled off of that bench. His heels and hips and head hit the floor like brick. He laid just like he fell.

This, of course, killed the spirit of the meeting for that night. Everybody was looking down at the drunk with more interest than they could possibly muster for the sermon, and I was purty disturbed too. We had a song and a dismissal prayer. The congregation gathered around the drunk man lying on the floor in the middle of the church. I walked back, pointed my finger in a stately-looking man's face, and says, "Sir, I'm deputizing you to take charge of this drunk." He was reluctant, but I persisted, and we got the boy taken into custody. People thought it might be dangerous for me to even stay in that country. But the boy later was converted and come into the church.

Not too long back I was over to the Ewing church in Virginia on a special occasion. The local preacher, Ray Crumley, warned me about some bad boys that had even rolled rocks out into the road at the foot of the hill and nearly caused some wrecks. He says, "They always come inside and wait till you start the sermon. Then they slip out and disturb while you preach."

I thought that all through. The service started and I sized up those boys in the back of the house. As Ray was leading the last verse of the last song before my scripture and prayer, I steps over and whispers, "Ray, have you got the church key?"

"Yes," he says.

"Give me the key, will ye?" says I. He handed me the key. I strode back the aisle, stuck it in the keyhole, and locked the door. I walked gently and with deliberation back to the pulpit and says quietly, "If anybody in the house wants out, I'll have to let 'em out. It anybody wants in, I'll have to let 'em in."

I read my text, had prayer, and preached. The boys were baffled and not unruly. When we were singing the last verse of the last hymn, I took the key out of my pocket, walked back the aisle, and unlocked the door. Then I came forward and handed Ray the key publicly and openly before the whole crowd. I had the benediction and let them go.

People told me there never was a case like it since Washington. I don't know. And maybe it's more of a discredit than a credit to me for having to do it. But I did it.

Many times, in preaching about how the Holy Spirit strives with us, I give this illustration that happened on my farm. In the fall of the year I always bring in the cattle. One rainy October day when there was a cold wind prevailing everywhere, I said to the boys that managed for me, "Go and bring down the cattle. It's cold. We'll put 'em in the stable." They herded them down and drove the whole crowd of them into the barnlot. The cattle hadn't hardly seen me for six months and they were a little wild all of them. We did, though, get them all in the big shed except one. An old stubborn steer wouldn't go in. He was afraid of everybody and watched everything everywhere. He raised his head and snorted and threatened. He had long horns.

I said to the boys, I says, "All of you git out of the way and let me handle 'im." I fetched a pan and dumped a little bran in it. The steer was in the barnlot, but he wouldn't go close to the shed. I took the pan and edged up toward him. The steer tromped right down into the corner of the barnlot. He surged around, and I had too much sense to go any closer: he showed fight. I set the bran down and backed off. The steer's countenance changed: he saw that bran, his ears drooped a little, he licked his chops, his eyes didn't look quite so wild. He made a step or two toward the pan, and with all the reach that his neck could do he barely touched his tongue to the bran. I picked it up and carried it along a little further. Reluctantly he follered.

I kept advancing the bran, and he kept a-coming. He follered me through the barnlot and down through the barn hall. At the back end of the hall I had a door open to a stable. I stepped over the threshold, sit the pan down in the middle of the stable, and clumb out over the manger. The steer had his head through the door, eyeing the bran. Finally, reluctantly, he raised up one foot and set it over the threshold; but he couldn't reach the pan. He stepped his other foot over; that gave him the reach, and he started licking at the bran. Forgetting all of his bullheadedness, he trailed his hind feet in over the threshold. We slammed the door shut. I picked up the bran, poured it in the manger, and he devoured it.

Now the bran is the Spirit. All men are wooed by the Holy Spirit, maybe a whole lifetime. That stubborn old steer could have follered the bran around the barnlot, through the bitter cold, or even into the barn, but always holding back a little, and finally fell prostrate and starved to death. But when he ate the bran, he had it. Before that he was just being moved by it. So with the Spirit and men.

Man disappointed God: he was worse than God thought he would be. And the devil got us by the tail in a downhill pull. But when Christ was born, the angelic bands caroled and sang, waltzing around on the clouds. He came to save us and break that downhill holt of the Devil. I say to people: All this thing that has been done for you, and are you going to let it all pass, disappoint God and Christ and the angels, and go on to hell anyway? How can you resist Him, dumber than that steer?

In 1936 I was preaching at the Nocona, Texas, church. The weather was 110° in the shade anywhere. The iron bedsteads was hot. The upholstering on a chair'd be so frying hot you couldn't lean against it.

There was a man attended that church every once in a while, and all the folks were interested in him. I went over to his house and said to him, "Mr. Dawson, my understanding is that you've gone through revival after revival and evangelist after evangelist for forty years, and you've turned everybody down. I'd like to have a special talk with you." He was friendly enough, and I hitched my chair over to his till it was right by his side. "Mr. Dawson," I says, "I understand you've never give any excuse, no reason, you've never told nobody; but I want to know why you don't accept Christ on the terms of the Gospel."

"Mr. Pritchett, I can't be saved."

"Why not?"

"I'm a murderer," he sighed.

"Murderer?" I said. "Did you kill somebody?"

He hesitated. "Well, since you asked me. I was raised in Alabama. I fell out with a neighbor of mine. He lived on a cotton field. His house was on a hillside. It was four steps from the ground up to the threshold. I opened my knife, walked up them steps, and knocked on his door to cut his head off."

"Well, what did you do?"

"I whetted my knife on his throat. He never said a d—d word. If he'd've let out one sound, I'd've cut it off. But someway or other my hand was stayed. I backed off of them steps and came to Texas. But I went there to kill him, which makes me a murderer just the same as if I had."

"Is that man living?" I asked.

"No, he's dead. And to make bad matters worse, my father fell out with me on that thing. And Daddy's dead."

I explained to him how "if we confess our sins, He is faithful and just to forgive us our sins and to cleanse us from all unrighteousness" and how "all manner of sin is forgiven except the sin against the Holy Ghost." When I said, "Get down here on your knees," he went down like a thousand bricks. I laid my hand on his head and shoulder and prayed fervently for him till he was in sobs and tears. I spent a lot of time on it. When I said, "Amen," he got back in his chair. He looked better and felt better. I says, "Will you come to church tonight?"

"Yes."

"Will you accept the call tonight?"

"I'll think about it."

I says, "You pray about it from now until then, and I hope you can get a conclusive answer. You've been truthful and honest before God. I'll see you tonight."

It was Sunday evening and the house was packed. I preached

with the best liberty I had had at all. I surveyed the crowd, but Mr. Dawson was not there. I gave an invitation for him if he was there; but he wasn't.

Monday night he wasn't there, and my feathers began to droop. But Tuesday night he showed up I preached and as soon as I give the invitation, this burly broad-shouldered man started to the front. He reached me his hand and fell down on his knees in front of the altar.

There was more than a dozen people to baptize in one of those pools out there. Everything in Texas has got a thorn on it or a thistle; even the grass has. Up on a big slick rock that led down toward the pool I pulled my shoes off. But between the rock and the edge of the water was a plot of stickery grass. I hung on around the necks of two brethren that had on shoes; I raised up my feet and got across the grass till I could touch the water, and waded on in till I found a good place. They came down one at a time, and I baptized Mr. Dawson into the church of Jesus Christ.

Chapter Eleven

INTO THE WATER

For many years the lower end of the church lot at French Broad was quite a wilderness. There were bushes and obsolete stumps; poke stalks, weeds, and blackberry briars grew up high as my head. I was down in there cleaning up, mowing with a mowing scythe, and I spotted a duck on a nest by the side of a stump. When I mowed up close, the duck spread her wings, stretched out her neck, and blew vehemently at me. I was a little cautious and generous toward her, so I left a few weeds around the nest, which had some fifteen eggs in it.

Next door to our church lived a local Baptist preacher named Moyers, who was road supervisor for our county. He and his wife and one daughter lived there. I knew they had three or four ducks and a pond in the barnlot, so I strolled on up to the house to talk with the wife. "Mrs. Moyers," I said, "there's a duck's nest out here in our church lot down among the poke stalks, and I'm not right sure whether they are Baptist ducks or Methodist ducks or Brethren ducks."

Those are the three churches and three constituencies of our Oak Grove Community, in sight and in hearing of each other across the valley so that on a clear day either one of them can hear the other one sing. "But," I says to her, "when the eggs hatch, I'll know for sure. If it's Methodist ducks and there comes up a rain, they'll take an umberell and go to a high hill to get out of the water. If it's Baptist ducks, Mrs. Moyers, they'll go down to your pond, turn around, and go in backwards. But if it's Brethren ducks, they'll come right to the water and plunge in head forward." I bid her goodbye and went back to my mowing.

When Mr. Moyers arrived home that evening, she said, "You know, Preacher Pritchett has been out here today," and she related the whole story.

Wriggling his fingers in his funny way, he says, "Madame, I'll tell you right now the preacher's got your ducks."

The eunuch was a-driving along. Philip was a young preacher, and the Spirit says to Philip, "You cut right over there and join yourself to that chariot." Philip was already baptized; he was already led by the Spirit. The eunuch wasn't.

And Philip spoke up and said, "Say, do you understand what you're readin', Nick?"

"No. It sure is strange stuff. I never will get onto it unless somebody explains it to me."

"Well," says Philip, "I'm a preacher. I'll try." And the record states that he "preached unto him Jesus." "Jesus, Jesus, Jesus, Jesus, Jesus"—is that all he said? If it was, Nick came up with a purty peculiar idea when he says, "See, here's water. What doth hinder me to be baptized?" How did he ever get onto that idea I wonder?

I don't know whether it was a creek or river or canal or pond or sluice or what; but the preacher said, "Well, now, Nick, if you really believe this with all your heart, you may." They stopped the chariot, tied up the mules, and the both of them waded down into the water, down in for more than a few drops. Philip baptized him, whereupon the Spirit carried Philip away, and the eunuch was carried away too with joy at receiving the Spirit.

If you read that scripture story and stand back and say, "I ain't a-gonna do it," the Spirit can't be leading you, that's sure.

At least ten methods of water baptism are being used around the world today. And a few years back I read in the newspaper of an eleventh method being introduced in Washington City, wherein a pastor called together something less than five hundred of his converts and with a single wholesale ceremony baptized the whole crowd with a garden hose. I suppose he thought they must have done that on Pentecost.

I sure do wish the Bible was more absolutely plain. Had I been the author of Matthew 28, I'd have handled it so that anybody would really be out of their head who couldn't see that a three-act forward dip immersion baptism was intended. But studying through the Bible passages and church history, triune immersion is the crystal-clear, scriptural, historical, gold-standard baptism.

When the early philosophers of the Church of the Brethren back in Germany in 1708 went to baptize in the River Eder, they soused them under, and folks that were just spectators would say, "Look at 'em dunking." So right from the start they were dubbed Dunker, Tunker, Täufer, the German words for Baptist. They are synonymous, three phases of the same name, like we say, good, better, best. Then there's the corrupted, spurious form "Dunkard," which is a mispronunciation and misapplication.

Alexander Mack, the establisher with seven others of the Church of the Brethren, was not a priest or a candidate for the priesthood like other reformers. He was not circumscribed by preconceived opinions. When he sprung, he sprung a long way. The first Tunkers were sticklers for the scripture and they had a diff cult time in Germany. They never had a church building in E rope. They had to resort to attics, cellars, or caves to worshi That's all in history verbatim and punctatinno.

Quakers are good people. William Penn was a Quaker. Year ing for a refuge from persecution, the Dunkers wrote Willia Penn a letter, and he wrote back and said, "Come on over, Bret ren, and we'll help you out." So over they practically all came an got in on the ground floor of America, half a century and eig years before the Declaration of Independence. Over here were lot of Baptists that had their origin in the British Isles, so th Dunkers were also referred to as German Baptists. Later on th name Church of the Brethren came to be used, which unfortu nately gets us confused with all the other kinds and kinds of kind of Brethren.

Mistress Roosevelt was a prominent woman in her day. And i Washington City she created a women's society to which the con gressmen's and the senators' wives and the vice-president's wif were admitted. She as the President's wife was the queen bee o the thing. They didn't eat much at their meetings, but she di serve tea or coffee and donuts. Mistress Roosevelt called it th Dunker Society. When I read that in the paper, I fell off of m chair, turned a sommerset, rolled out the door, ran around th house several times, and come back in to read it over again. I di enjoy that so much. I figured the First Lady of the land ha joined my church, and we'd now have a national church in Washington City.

As a boy I never heard of a baptistry And they've been purty uncommon during much of my ministry. I've had some strange baptisms and some frigid baptisms. One of the most pronounced cases was when I was holding a revival at the Walnut Grove church in Taylor's Valley, Virginia, not far from the North Carolina line. There was a sweeping revival, and a half a dozen were new applicants for baptism. White Top Creek, dashing down from White Top Mountain, made a pool purty close to the church where the water poured down and scooped out a large pool, then stood eddy and ran on away.

When we went there for the baptizing, the cliffs by the side of that pool had icycles bigger than I am, six and eight and ten feet high a-hanging on the walls. The ice on the pool was three inches thick. Men worked with maddox and axes, chopped a groove around, and broke out the block, leaving a hole four foot square. They fished out the chunks of ice and laid them on top.

The zero hour for the baptizing had come. Two men grasped me one by each arm and stood me chest-deep down through the ice into the water. I was getting acclimated to it and they brought a woman and helped her down in. I had the ceremony, put her under once and twice and thrice, and had the prayer. They lifted her out, she left for warm shelter, and I proceeded till we got the group baptized.

But just as they were ready to hoist me out of the ice, another woman walked down that had never made an demonstration at the church, never made any announcement, and she asked to be baptized. Her hair hung loose down her back to her waist. The other women had protected themselves a little bit with ice-caps and gum coats; but she didn't have either. I asked her some questions, they eased her down into the freezing water, and I baptized her. Before she could get to the house, her hair froze in long icycle strings.

Now that I'm old and tottery, folks worry over me and ask, "Brother Pritchett, aren't you afraid to go in the water?" They say that even about a baptistry. No, not one bit I'm not. I'm not afraid to venture down through the ice again any time. Never in my life have I known a single person to ever sneeze after a baptism—either applicant or administrator. That's a stubborn fact. I'd baptize a man if I had a severe cold; I'd pay no attention to that, not a bit in the world. Is that faith, or am I foolish?

An administrator in a triune immersion baptism ought to understand thoroughly what he is doing and execute it gracefully and with effort. When a young preacher is fixing to do his first baptizing, I give him some instructions. It should be gone into with as much skill and concentration as ever a physician had delivering a child.

Here, for instance, was how we did it at the last baptizing we had at the French Broad church. The woman had never been baptized before. I always read Matthew 18, emphasizing about going to your brother or your sister if you get into a fuss. I took her affirmation to that. I drilled her on some things and said, "We like to be clean Christians. We don't make it a test of fellowship, but we certainly advise against smoking and drinking, the use of tobacco and such grubby habits as that." I rehearse other doctrines like not going to war and following the foolish fashions of the world. I says, "I'm not asking you do do what I do. But rather, are you willing to be as plain as the Bible is on these questions?"

She nodded: "Yes."

"The Lord has heard you," I told her. And I says to the assembled congregation, "Jesus warns us, 'Despise not one of these that's comin' in.' Twenty minutes from now this woman is gonna be reborn, and you're her elder sister or brother in the Kingdom."

The water in the baptistry was chilly, pumped straight out of the ground. When she got to the edge, I said, "Just come right on down." I reached up a hand and led her down the steps into the water. Our French Broad baptistry has a platform for younger people that is ten or fifteen inches higher than the main bottom. I had explained to her before, and I says, "You're on the platform and in your case you'll step off of it." I held her hand and let her step down to the lower level. I says, "You're not uneasy, you don't dread the water, do you?"

"No."

"Well, that's fine."

I reached down, dipped up a little water, and said, "Dip up a little water in your hands and put some on your face." She did. I said to her, "You kneel right down, right where you are." I helped her and she did. If the water isn't deep enough for long gangling men or women when they kneel—it ought to be up to the middle of the chest—I say, "Sit back on your haunches," and that gets them six inches deeper, in the same pool. And you can baptize just as well.

When this woman kneeled, she was deep enough but she went forward a little bit, and we was too close to the ledge. I said, "Scoot back a little." The buoyancy of the water and her effort and me together, we scooted her slightly back so we'd be sure not to hit the ledge. I dipped up a handful of water and poured it down the back of her neck, right down the spinal column. That knocks the chill off.

Then I got a good handful of her garments right between the shoulders; I got a firm holt there, I always do. Just to lay your hand on, you don't have your applicant completely in charge. Be sure you have a good holt on the garments right between the shoulders, a bit toward the neckline. Now I said, "Mary, I'm gonna do this service; I'm gonna do the baptizing. You just submit to it. You'll have a chance to get your breath between each dip, and there's three dips." I'd told her this before we went in, for that matter.

I says, "You just dip some water and put your hands on your face." She did. I placed my free hand over hers and said, "Dost thou truly believe that Jesus Christ is the Son of God, and that he brought from heaven a saving Gospel?"

"Yes," she answered.

"Dost thou willingly renounce Satan, with all his pernicious ways, and all the sinful pleasures of this world?"

"Yes."

"Dost thou covenant with God through Christ Jesus to live a life of obedience from now until death? Can you say Yes to that, Mary?"

"Yes."

"Upon this, thy confession of faith which thou hast made before God and these witnesses, thou shalt, for the remission of thy sins, be baptized in the name of the Father," and with the handholt at the shoulders and a hand over her face I immersed her once, giving her then a chance to breathe and nod when ready; "and of the Son" with a second immersion; "and of the Holy Spirit" with a third.

Hands crossed on the head of the applicant, I give the closing prayer: "All-wise God, our heavenly Father, we look up unto thee and ask thee to look down in tender mercy upon this thy handmaid which has just been baptized into a covenant relationship with thee. Wouldst thou forgive all the past and enroll her name in the Lamb's Book of Life and give to her the leadership of the Holy Spirit. Amen."

Chapter Twelve

THE LORD GIVES THE INCLINATION

Lately I said to a young fellow who was about to decide for or against the ministry and was about to decide not, because he's not right sure of himself, I says: "I don't want you to make a misfit; it'd be a shame to make a misfit. If you haven't got the call, if you're not a minister, you can't do it—effectively. And if you've got the call and you don't heed it, you'll be a misfit wherever you go, and you'll never get it completely off of your mind." I've seen men after fifty years old desert what they were a-doing and enter the ministry.

I'd ask you this: Does preaching appeal to you? Does it look heroic to you? Can you sit in the pew and wish you could do that? I don't go to horse races, but did you ever see a horse when the jockey's holding him when it's his turn to get in the race? It takes two men to hold the horse while the jockey jumps on. He's raring and surging and pitching against the bits. He loves to run. Have you got that? Is the Gospel brandfire news to you? Is it the most incredibly marvelous thing in the world? If so, back in there somewhere is the original call coming up in the gamut of your being.

The ministry is not a financial scheme. It is not a matter of palace cars, deep carpet, steak dinners. There's gonna be a lot of sacrifice, such as goes with anything worthwhile. You won't make any money. You might possibly balance accounts. You will, though, be thrown in good society.

If you're a called minister, it don't matter much about peculiarities in your speech, whether you're fast or slow or high or low. If the Lord gives the inclination, he'll provide a voice with which you can reach your people. I'm sure of that because I've seen so many varieties.

In preaching it's not good usually to let somebody else have all the preliminaries and then you pop up and take over to preach. At least while they're singing the last song ahead of your sermon, you'd better be in the pulpit standing, and during the four or five verses find your audience, see who's there and who you've met already and whether Aunt Susie got her accustomed place. Take in your audience and look about you. There's nothing else you've got to do, so while they're singing, you get your audience in your mind. If there's a water pitcher in your way or a glass tumbler, move it out of reach so you won't knock it off accidentally. Settle your mind, find your equilibrium, and as the singing fades, start out your message in a firm low tone. When you preach, look at them; show your countenance. And be sure you stand on both feet. Don't swamp. Cover the ground. Take charge of your service and of your audience; that's half the battle. Your message should be fundamental, historical, philosophical, and biblical. Begin. Be brief. Be seated.

If you're embarrassed or there's anything wrong, try not to let your audience know it. Let them continue their good opinion. I saw a boy preaching one time and he unbuttoned his coat and buttoned his coat, unbuttoned his coat and buttoned his coat fifty times during his sermon. He was embarrassed. If you're scared and you let the audience know about it, you'll have a cool service. On some occasions though, anybody is sure to have an off day preaching. It's awful when it's like that. You're a scarecrow talking to statues and praying to an unknown God. But there is no experience quite to equal when your audience merges, their minds fusing with yours, and they pull the preach out of you and the Spirit broods over his own. It's profound.

Some days I don't need my notes any more than I need a dose of oil. And sometimes I preach scripturally, read a verse and explain it, read another and so on. That was the old way. Take the twelfth chapter of Romans; every verse is a sermon. You read a verse, explain some, read another and explain, and another, and purty soon you've got in thirty minutes or forty and it's time to quit. My favorite chapters to preach on are John 5, Hebrews 1 and 9, Revelations 20 and 21.

In funeral sermons, no matter who it is, I don't tag him for hell, but neither do I shove him through the Pearly Gates. I hit the middle of the road. If he's done some outstanding things, I mention them. But nobody is perfect and if you make a spotless saint out of anybody, folks can easily criticize or figure they don't have to be any better than that. I make out a line of notes for every funeral, using a lot of things that was in the othern; but I make every one fit the person. When Bill Melvin died, who had the old mill and blacksmith shop, he left two sisters behind. As a very young preacher I was called in and I hit upon the text about Lazarus and Martha and Mary.

When you go to preaching back in the hills, you've got to mind your P's and Q's, or you'll ruin everything. Don't make embarrassing breaks like asking, "Who's that old ball-headed man with the big nose?"

"That's my father."

Wouldn't that be too bad? You'd drop your candy right there. In some churches all the folks is kin, and no matter how queer somebody is, you can't say anything about it without saying it to his brother or his cousin.

Suppose you're back in the mountains of Kaintucky and they tell you, you can go down there to the spring and wash. They don't have a bathroom; they don't have any washpans neither. An old preacher I knew was visiting in North Carolina and they sent him to wash at the spring. He douses his hair and face and beard there in the branch. He gets up, blinks through the water, and yells, "Where's the towel, or ain't you got any?"

He just ruined himself right there.

The Church of the Brethren has all the things in it that any church has and a lot of things that no church has. And one of the latter is the full Love Feast that reproduces everything that happened in the Upper Room—the feetwashing, the spiritual fellowship meal, and finally the communion. I was schooled in the way the old Brethren did it. I think it's biblical, historical, and worshipful; and I like the custom of it.

For the self-examination service somebody reads 1 Corinthians 11; I always have that read. Then we read the thirteenth chapter of John about Jesus washing his disciples' feet. I sit at the head of the table if I'm officiating. I let somebody across the table from me wash my feet. I wash the feet of the next fellow, put on my shoes, and proceed to offer a defense of feetwashing, how it is for humility and service and cleansing, and how Jesus commanded it so clear and strong.

The scriptures is specific and plain out as to bread and wine for the communion but not about the fellowship meal that comes before. We have a variety as to whether there's beef or mutton or whatever. During World War II, when you couldn't buy beef except with ration points, we at French Broad overstepped that by getting a dozen big hens. We hanged our great old cook pot on a chain, plopped in the chickens, and boiled them tender. The deacons'd tangle through that, fish out the backs and legs, dish out the meat, send it all the way around the tables, and we'd eat chicken. I've been to Love Feast where there was fried chicken, doughnuts, pancakes, pies. I observed one fraternal method where they'd stack four pies up on one plate, slice down through them all, and pass the variety around. Most of the Love Feasts you go to now, though, are simpler and have just beef, broth soup, and bread.

But when I come to the communion proper, I'm bound. It wouldn't do at all to have Coca Cola or apple cider or chocolate milk for communion wine, or potatoe cakes or a dodger of fluffy cornbread to stand for Christ's broken body. It's to be unleavened bread. It doesn't have to taste so good, though I relish it when it does. But the bread should be unleavened. And for drink it's got to be the product of the grape. I'm not in a fuss with anybody whether it's juice or fermented.

At the beginning of the fellowship meal in the middle of the service I always say, "Now all of the children, bring them to the table and give them something to eat." So they join in partly on that. And after the communion is over, I call the children and break off a piece of the unleavened bread for every child and have a little explanation but no ceremony. Little children can be profoundly influenced by Love Feasts.

The capsheaf of the Bible ordinances is the anointing service. Up in Ohio once a Brother Coffman, I think his name was, took me around by the hospital to visit his granddaughter. Soon as we entered the room, she went to crying mournfully. He tried to console her, but she kept crying right out. She was about twelve or thirteen years old. After we left, I inquired more about her. Something had gone wrong with her bones, and the ball-and-socket femur that goes up in the pelvis bone had snapped right off. The lower part of her body was pressed in a cast, and a rope to her foot with a big weight kept her leg stretched out. The doctors said it would be a year before she would walk—if she ever did. The child was weeping not because she was so bad sick but because she wanted to go home.

The grandfather was very anxious that the girl be anointed. Her parents paid little attention to the church. But the girl had turned to Christ in a revival the year before. Brother Coffman and the grandmother and myself talked it over and went again to the hospital. I hitched my chair up to the child's bed, and I says, "How're you feeling today, Mary?" She was smiling a little bit.

"Mary," I says, "Have you been baptized?"

"Yes, sir." And she told me when.

I says, "Have you ever communed? Have you ever been at the communion where they wash feet and eat together?"

"Yes, in October I was there."

"Did you set by Grandma?"

"Yes," she said, and grandma just cried out.

"Well, Mary, there's another scripture; I don't know whether you ever heard it. Did you ever hear about that scripture where if you've got sickness, you're anointed with oil?''

She'd heard about it. "Did you ever see it done?'' No, she didn't believe she had. I made a little explanation about faith and healing and forgiveness and let it up to Mary to decide. She definitely wanted to be anointed.

I walked down to the end of the hall to the head nurse. "Mrs. Sellenbarger,'' I says, or whatever her name was, "I'm Brother Pritchett, and Brother Coffman is here, the grandfather of Mary Coffman. We're having a religious service in Mary's room, an anointing service for healing, and we'd sure like you to come up and be present. And besides that, have you got any olive oil or sweet oil in your cabinet?''

"Yes, I have,'' she said. I always ask them to furnish the oil. It gets them involved. She reached up and got me a bottle of olive oil. Actually I had a bottle in my grip. But I ask them for it; then they're in on the thing. So Mrs. Sellenbarger came along.

Mary's grandfather waited on me, and we anointed her with oil for the healing of her body. He gave me a drop or two of oil and I applied it with the words, "I anoint thee with oil in the name of the Lord for the strengthening of thy faith.'' I held out my hands for another supply: "And with oil in the name of the Lord for the comforting of thy conscience,'' and another application. "And with oil in the name of the Lord for the full assurance of the forgiveness of all shortcomings and the possible healing of the body.''

Then I laid my hand on her head, and Brother Coffman laid a hand on, and I my other hand, and he his. (But right there's a place you've got to be mighty careful: you have a sick body. I've had men that wasn't cautious; they'd lay a heavy hand on the head and unthinkingly bear down. So I always put my hand first, barely let it tip, and hold up the weight of anybody else's hands from pressing down on the frail body.) I had fervent prayer for Mary and challenged the Lord on his anointing scripture to forgive and heal.

Say, that girl in a short time was on her feet and threw away that cast. The doctors thought she would have to stay in bed for at least a year and probably wouldn't ever be all right then. But it all healed fine and that girl grew up and married and become a mother.

Chapter Thirteen

"ALL CREATURES GREAT AND SMALL"

My mother related many a time how she cried and lamented about her pet rat. Grandfather, in cleaning out the crib, found a nest of big fat little baby rats. He gave her one of the chunky fellows, and she carried it to the house. She put it in with the mother cat and her baby kittens. The cat, instead of devouring the rat, suckled it, and took care of it along with her own babies. The little rat slept and romped and sucked right with the kittens. But Grandmother figured that was bad business, so she took the baby rat out and killed it. Mother cried and cried.

I was born in the Crouch house. Soon after my birth Father bought a farm without any buildings, and in a year or two he built a house. His first effort at a barn was to split out long poles in the woods, much longer than fence rails, set up two pens with a space between, and roof that over.

An old mother rabbit crept into that barn when snow was on the ground, which is earlier than little rabbits are born usually, and dug down between the stalks next to the partition between two cow stables. And there she lined a nest with the fur of her own body and deposited her brood. Mother in milking the cow discovered them. At intervals she and Father took me through the snow and cold up to the barn. He'd reach down, gently bring out the baby rabbits, and show them to me. I can see them yet, cuddled there in Daddy's hand, and that's been more than eighty years ago.

In the deep of winter John Carathers felled a tree that had a squirrel in it. He caught the squirrel and gave it to us children—a wild squirrel right out of the woods.

Mother noticed that the squirrel was pregnant. I didn't know it nor none of us children. Daddy drove a nail in the edge of the mantle and hung the cage close to the fire every night so the baby squirrels, when they were born, wouldn't get too cold. In the daytime, with the house warmer, we could just set the cage back in the room anywhere. One February night the old mother gave birth to four tiny squirrels. After they had grown a bit, we'd take those baby squirrels to bed with us. They'd crawl everywhere, crawl all over us, cuddle down for warmth. They wouldn't bite.

And that old mother squirrel she'd let you reach right in there and pull them out from under her. She was a wild squirrel to begin with; she was not petted when she was young. But she learned that we were not going to harm her babies. We raised every one of them little squirrels. Daddy built a great big cage out in the yard up on posts, screened it all around, and put a wheel in for them to race and spin around in. Later, though, we let them run loose. Those squirrels stayed close by at first, but kept getting a little further and little further away.

Father was a-working at his carpenter's bench in the spring of the year, and John and I, we were with him up about the barn, when a hawk swooped down, picked up a chicken, a purty good-size chicken, from an old hen's brood, and sailed away with it. He was downhill to go, and that was advantage to him. But that plucky old hen just riz and flew right at the tail of the hawk, chasing after him down toward Knob Creek.

Father lit out hollering and me and John a-follering. We raced down a quarter of a mile, when to our amazement we met the hen and chicken heading back to the barnlot, the hen a-clucking and her chick frisking from one side of the path to the other. The chick was wounded, but not beyond being able to keep up with the mother hen. The hawk had a holt on the chicken enough to carry it, but he hadn't probed deep enough to kill it. And with that hen on his tail he had to drop the chicken. It's a rare hen can fly like that. A Plymouth Rock couldn't. But this old bird was good on wings. And through a great excitement and in view of a loss of her brood she did the almost impossible.

I have many such instances of what animal parents have done to save their young. Greater still is the affection of human parents and what they have gone through for their children. And supreme is how Jesus Christ suffered and died to rescue the human creation from the opposing enemy, the devil.

I want the goodwill of wild life. I hate to have a quail or bird or squirrel be on his toes all the time trying to get away from a monster that's gonna kill him. I'd rather have his goodwill and let him know he's in safe hands. Feeding birds in bad weather when the snow is heavy on the ground, I can walk out gently, pitch the cracked corn down, and the birds won't hardly get out of the way. They'll hop straight up to me for the corn. I've had as many as thirty-two cardinals out under the sugar tree at the same time. But if I was around shooting at them, they'd fly a half a mile away and hide in the woods. They know the difference. Squirrels do too. If I took to killing them, they'd flee for the woods. But they stay where they're favored. All animals do that, even fish. Foxes'll get clever and tame if you don't run them with dogs.

Colonel A. R. Swann was a millionaire of this community. He had a vast estate of five thousand acres and seventy-five tenants. He was a businessman, a church promoter, a good citizen in every way. There was some sport about him, and he loved to shoot geese out in the bottoms of his farm. One time he hitched up a yoke of oxen and lay on the wagon tongue between them so as to approach some geese. When he got in shooting range, he let the oxens come to a halt. He pulled down on the geese and blazed away. The oxens run wild with him all tangled up in there and Colonel Swan barely escaped getting trampled and mangled. But he was very happy to have killed a goose.

They look better to me alive.

Even when you're feeding the cows, they don't know any better than to steal the hay as you carry it along, discommoding you a lot, throwing you off of your equilibrium so you can hardly get the hay carried, with the cows grabbing at it. But it's better far to let a cow do that and have goodwill toward you than to turn around and beat and rend her and make her scared of you. She in her mind has a low appreciation of you when you act like that. The same way with a horse or any animal.

Traveling in the West once, driving through one of those broad flat states, we were looking for a place to eat our lunch. The weather was scalding hot. We came to a culbert where a little creek went through. The water flowing off the concrete bottom of the culbert had scooped out quite a pond. When we had our sandwiches purty well consumed, the question developed, what to do with the garbage. I said, "Let me have the crumbs. The fish is praying for food." My travel companions laughed at that. I took the crumbs and pieces over and dropped them down. The fish flashed right up to the top and gulped them in. Who knows but what in their field of thought they were hungry and yearning to get food from some source? And we answered their prayer. They didn't understand it, but neither do we understand God.

The earth is a massive playhouse of Jehovah's mountains and plains, oceans and deserts, full of his birds and animals, insects and fish. All of them is God's creation and we are his custodians.

Cutting hay once, I saw a terrapin carrying along on the mowing machine. One of the guards had stuck right in between its neck and foreleg, way in. I stopped the machine quick and rescued the badly injured terrapin. By morning it was swelled so stiff it couldn't get in the shell nor out; it was about halfway in and halfway out. The only thing we had to do, if it was not vitally hurt, was to keep the flies away, which we did. That sore place healed up and the creature got quite tame.

Another time, as I was mowing, I heard something crunch. I looked back and the mowing machine had rolled right over a terrapin; the cogs of the wheel had crushed him down flat, but not plumb flat. I jumped off and picked him up. His legs and head was sprawled out. He was helpless. The shell was shattered into little sections, oblong and all kinds of shapes. I took my pocketknife and begin to set the shell, gently prying the fragments. You could see and hear the blood suck. I arched the shell all up and set it as nice as I could.

My youngest daughter Evelyn brought me out a bucket of water after a while, and I sent the terrapin back to the house. We lodged him down in the cool of the basement. He had to set perfectly still; he couldn't crawl a bit. In two or three days he began to show improvement. The cracked places started healing over like a new fingernail growing. A week later though, I noticed at one spot a bit of ooze seeping out. I took a feather and a drop or so of turpentine, riled it in that place, did that two or three times, and a couple of creepers, maggots, scooted out. In spite of all our precaution a blowfly had got in and blowed him anyhow. There wasn't, though, but two or three of the creepers, and when I got them coaxed out, the spot healed up and the feller became a real pet. He'd eat right out of your hand: worms, soft bread, banana peelings, cantalope, watermelon, rotten apples. He wasn't afraid, not a bit afraid. After he was entirely recuperated, we carried him back to his usual haunts and turned him loose. That's been twenty-five years and I've never seen him since. I hope he didn't take rheumatism or some other ill akin to that crush and die on account of it.

I've found terrapins with mud caked so thick under them that they couldn't reach ground for a footing. It would be after a heavy dew or light rain, and moist dirt in plowed or cultivated soil would keep sticking fast. Hot sunshine and starvation soon puts an end to the poor creature. Whenever I've found them in this perdicament, I've peeled off the cake of dirt and seen them crawl away almost smiling.

Incredible is God's ingenuity among his animal creation. For nigh onto fifty years I've been saving newspaper articles about animals. I have two massive scrapbooks just on them. But many remarkable things I've observed myself.

The foxes once carried away all my chickens from a roost in the coop except one old yellow hen that flew off and found her a safe place up in the hay mow. At the time two of my three cats had disappeared, leaving one lonely old black tomcat. That hen and the tom soon began to get real affectionate. The old yellow hen would stand still and let the cat rub all around her. The tom would love the hen's neck and head. The cat made all the advances, but the hen showed no fear. When the cat laid down in sun or shade, the lonely hen would stand by or nestle down close to him. Here was a mammal and a fowl that took up together.

But tomcats can be cruel, even to their own young. As long as a mother cat suckles her kittens, she won't come back in heat. Tomcats know this and may kill the babies so the mother will dry up and come back in heat quick. Squirrels'll do that too.

The second time I was supposed to go to Europe on a cattle boat, a number of us found ourselves day after day congregated in the lobby of a Norfolk hotel waiting for a longshoremen's strike to get stopped. In one of our many open forums we got to discussing insects: wasps, hornets, mud daubers, trap-door spiders. We southern boys from Tennessee, North Carolina, and Virginia brought up the barnlot tumblebug.

We rehearsed how this remarkable bug finds a suitable deposit of fecal matter, makes her a ball, lays eggs in it, and rolls and rolls the ball until it is perfectly round and nice and smooth. The northern boys, especially the New England boys, they listened with interest until we got to chirping in and describing how the male and the female engages together and cooperates together rolling their prize ball of manure, how the one rides the ball in such a fashion as to keep it topheavy in the direction they're traveling and the other is behind it backing along pushing the ball with its hind legs till they bury it in a hole where the eggs can hatch and have choice nourishment.

One of the New England boys, a long, spare, gangling fellow, rose to his feet and with a considerable amount of slang roared, "I don't believe my own lies!" and stomped out. All of us southern boys horselaughed. The doubter returned after a spell, we started discussing again about tumblebugs playing ball, and he stomped right out again. We never were able to make him believe that there's such a thing as this clown of the southern barnlot, this architect of the dung heap.

The snake is the most despised of all created creatures. All snakes have a bad name, worse than any other animals in all God's creation. But a snake is clean; he won't eat anything that's dead. If he finds a dead bird or a dead mouse or any decomposing corpse, he doesn't devour it. He wants his food alive.

I've had a number of pet black snakes. They are easy to handle, really. Be gentle, easy, quiet. Don't rush, don't make quick or long gestures, and perhaps the snake will lay still and let you pick it up and sleek its curving body. Most animals like to be sleeked. I have a bunch of cattle, some of which are just tame and gentle enough until they'll stand and let me scratch them. I scratch them on the head or a place on the back where they can't reach, and they'll twist and lean against me; they enjoy it. We used to have hogs, and if you scratch a hog, he'll lift his foot and hold it up there so you can scratch better. You move over to the other side and he'll raise the other leg to invite some scratching there.

We have old rusty-looking lizards on the fences, stumps, dead logs. Many a time I've taken a stalk of grass, slipped up to a lizard, and tickled him a little bit, and he'd raise up each leg in turn to let me scratch him. How well black snakes like to be tickled and sleeked I don't know, but they yield to it all right. You have to be careful though, because if you move suddenly, he'll coil for a strike.

I have great respect for anything God created, no matter what it is. And I try to find out how it fits into the scheme of things. No woman likes to have her winter coat all messed up with mud daubers' nests, and no man appreciates finding a mud dauber's nest under the collar of his overcoat. But if you had all of the daubers destroyed, one scientist said that the spiders would run us off the earth between April and October, unless we had something else to combat them with. Mud daubers and wasps are God's way of combating spiders and keeping balance.

The many varieties of daubers build a clay or dirt or mud cocoon. They ketch a spider, put him in the bottom of the cocoon, give the spider an anesthetic, and lay an egg on him. They fetch more spiders, anesthetize them all, fill up the cocoon, and seal it tight. The egg that's on the bottom spider hatches out. Each spider is dead asleep, well-preserved, and fine nourishment as the young dauber devours them one by one. On a number of occasions I've broken open the mud cocoon and let the spiders be exposed to the air. The anesthetic will evaporate away, and the spiders go on and live and spin webs again.

We were hauling hay in the summertime, and I was setting the hayfork when I heard the womenfolks screaming down at the house. "Come down here, Reuel! Hurry, Daddy, come quick!" Ella and the girls were shouting.

I leaped off the hay and raced down, thinking the house was on fire. "Whatsa matter, whatsa matter?" I asked.

"Oh, lookee here what a big snake."

It was a blowing viper, a spreading adder, about two feet and a half long. A blowing viper that long is big to its length, and the spots make a lot of people mistake them to be a rattlesnake. He had a considerable swell-place in his body and was sorta trying to crawl sideways. I'm not a snake handler, nor I certainly wouldn't do it from any tempting standpoint. But I'm not afraid of snakes, so I just walked over and picked him up. I was purty sure this undue large spot in his body was something he had swallowed. Holding the viper's head out a little from one hand, I pressed my other thumb and index finger right behind that lump and began easing it forward. When I got within about six inches of his mouth, he realized something was a-gonna happen; he opened up and out dropped a common hoptoad bigger around by far than he was. The toad was all slimy and cramped together, but I could notice slight signs of life. I carried him over, dunked him in the rainbarrel, and washed the slime off. In a few minutes the toad began to bat his eyes a little. A few more minutes and he was setting up a bit. And before long he was able to hop short hops. I took him over to where a hole went through the rough wall foundation of the house, and he made his getaway.

That poor hoptoad was overwhelmed, hopelessly lost, with nothing whatever he could do on his part. He had been no match in strength and cunning to the cruel, hungry serpent. He was doomed, forever doomed, unless there would be a super-intelligence intervene. In like manner we of the human family were overwhelmed and hopelessly, everlastingly lost—and God intervened. Christ did for me exactly what I did for that hoptoad. He rescued me from the Serpent. He delivered me. He saved me.

When the toad got out of the snake's body, he was for the time being *safe*—though I wouldn't use the word *saved.* I didn't kill that snake. I walked over across the road and pitched him in the field. The toad will have to watch out because that snake and many other snakes are still hungry. He's safe, and he'll have to keep safe.

Chapter Fourteen

ONE OF A KIND

I thank the Lord for my individuality that I was born with, endowed with, inherited. It's been said to me already, "There never was but a baker's dozen of Reuel B. Pritchetts, and you are all fourteen of them." I don't know what he meant by that. People introduce me and say, "We'll hear Brother Pritchett in his style." I'm not conscious of it; I hardly know it, though I guess some of the things I say are local, so very local that they're really mine. But everybody is different; God makes each of us individual if we don't stifle it, and I've tried not to.

But there's a number of stories got started about me that are false and untrue. On an occasion or so I've taken a piece of wood maybe five foot long, stuck one end in the fireplace with the other end on the woodbox, and as it burnt off, pushed it on in. I'd get it burnt up before bedtime. Now somebody saw me do that, and the story spread all around everywhere: "Brother Pritchett don't cut his wood at all. He burns rails, burns 'em full length, and jist feeds 'em into the fire." I'm not that lazy. I chop cords and cords of wood every winter.

I. N. H. Beahm, who preached during the lightning storm at the Bristol Annual Conference in 1905, visited me last when he was eighty-seven. Before breakfast he'd go out, grab a sledge hammer, and whoum, whoum, whoum, pound on a big stump for a while. Then he'd run up to a limb and chin himself a couple dozen times. I. N. H. Beahm was a great observer of health, and he'd have lived to be a hundred if an automobile driven by a drunk hadn't crashed into the automobile he was in and killed him at ninety-one. Well, I'm not that spry; but with the cattle and birds and chopping my wood I get plenty of exercise.

I've retained my own individuality in my spelling, though you might not guess it from this book which has been polished up considerable. Spelling was always a little hard for me. A word that has three syllables, I cut corners and leave out the middle syllable, and a lot of times I'm puzzled over whether you start with an *i* or an *e* on a word. And even if you've got it on your mind right, you may hit the wrong key and put it wrong. If I've got to major on the language and orthography and grammar, plus the typewriting, it all piles up on me and I lose the gist of what I'm struggling to express. I can do punctuation by concentrating a lot; but if I do that, I won't get the article done. I can retype an article correcting all the minor points, but that takes twice as long as to edit the story down in the first place.

My handwriting is something to behold also. I have boxes and boxes of valuable records stacked away at my place with the writing so bungled up that you couldn't read them if everything was in boxcar letters—because I wrote it. There's only one man living that could read them and nary a man dead.

It's a sort of retribution I guess that people continually misspell my first name. They write it Revel (which I rather like), Rule, Rhul, Rural, Reull, Reuell, Reurel, Rool, and every possible sort of way. How did I come to have this name? There was a man that was a friend of my father by the name of Reuel Maydon. Daddy liked the man and liked the name. He looked it up and it's a Bible name, and that's how I got it. Moses had two father-in-laws, and one of them was Reuel.

Birth, salvation, marriage, and death are four things that happen to any normal human being, and we should be at our best for either of the occasions. The first three have come to me in that order. Marriage has come and gone. The fourth is soon to come, and then birth will be gone, but not salvation.

I had a good marriage and a faithful helpmeet. Ella stayed more at home. She freely let me roam around. But we had a world of fun in our family. Giving medicine, for instance, was always an acrobatic event. We gave home remedies like Epsom salts, castor oil, turpentine, cod liver oil, quinine, all of which was very repulsive to the taste. No medicine that I know of has a good taste. I'd hold the youngster, who'd sniff, cry, twist, squirm, kick, scream, and put up a real fight. Ella would thrust in the spoon and pour the medicine down, with the child spluttering and bluttering. It was always a major upheaval in the peace of the family.

Well, one day I got sick myself. I tipped Ella off how to handle it. She called the four children together and says, "Now, children, we have to give Daddy some castor oil, and I really dread trying to give it to him. You know how bad it tastes." Yes, sir, they knew very well. She says, "I expect I'll have to have some help. I want you all to come in with me, and we'll work together. He's awful contrary, and he's gonna be mean to get that oil down him." She posted them good.

In she comes with a chubby bottle and a big spoon. And I *was* sick, setting in my rocking chair in front of the fireplace. She says, "Daddy, you'll have to take some castor oil."

"No, no, I don't want no castor oil."

"No, now you've got to take it. You need the oil."

"You're not a-gonna give me no oil. I'd rather be sick than take it. I hate that stuff."

She argued with me, and I'd argue too. She poured out a brimming spoonful and brought it toward my mouth. I began to shiver and shake and sour and frown and scold. She says, "Children, you get a-holt of him here now. Gomer, you grab this leg here, and, Ethel, you take that one." Erlene caught holt of one hand, and Evelyn, she was little, she grasped the other one. As the spoon loomed nearer, I was twisting ever way to get out from under it, kicking my legs vehemently, slapping my leg-holders against each other, contorting my arms and tossing my arm-holders to and fro around the big chair. Ella was shouting, "Swaller it. Swaller it. Don't you dare spit it out. If you don't swaller it good, we'll give you another dose. Children, hold him tight." It was a heroic occasion. The children did their very best. Ella hit my mouth. I spluttered and finally gulped down the castor oil. I got every drop of it.

"Well, that's done," Ella says. "You can let loose now, children."

They turned all holts loose and began brushing the dust off, buttoning up their clothes, smoothing back their hair, and taking credit for the operation. The little one says, "We made him take it, didn't we, Momma?" The children was in complete earnest; this was the one opportunity they had in a lifetime to get even with their parents for pouring down them all those old bad-tasting medicines they couldn't see any good reason for doing.

We'd have hogs' feet for company once in a while. Boys'd come home with Gomer from school. We'd be at the table and I'd say to the boy setting right next to me: "Would you have a hog's foot?"

He'd say, "Yes."

I'd balance a piece on my fork and ask, "Hind foot or fore foot?" I'd challenge him for an answer.

He delicately says, "Hind foot."

So I lay that piece down and get another—and I myself wouldn't know the difference. Ethel and Erlene and Evelyn and Gomer would just preach my funeral for pulling a joke like that.

Through the years I've had a lot of inquiries about the use of tobacco. That's a puzzle all right. And I'm from the tobacco belt myself. On the one hand, I. N. H. Beahm used to preach that if God intended for man to smoke he'd have put a chimley spouting out the top of his head, or he'd have turned his nose downside up so it would be a chimley. And there was the man who asked a minister whether a person that chewed tobacco could go to heaven. The minister answered right back: "If he went to heaven chewing tobacco, he'd have to go to hell to spit."

But on the other hand there's a couple of places in the Bible that support the use of tobacco. I hate to admit it, but I'm honest enough to point the places out to people who smoke and chew if the Bible justifies them in their habit. The one verse is in the very last chapter of the Bible in the book of Revelations: "He which is filthy, let him be filthy still." And I found another one too. The Apostle Peter wrote that we are to eschew evil. I pondered and meditated that thing through, and as far as I can imagine, tobacco is the evilest thing we can chew!

Chapter Fifteen

TO COLLECT AND CONSERVE

As far back as I can remember, I've been inclined to collect and conserve. Through seventy some years I've accumulated an immense conglomeration, a mixed multitude. Collecting has been my passion, so much so that my children and even my wife were never able to quite understand. It looked like Daddy's going crazy. Maybe he'd lose his mind. "We can't even get in and out of the house, it's so full of stuff."

It was full all right. The rooms was packed, the porches were crowded with counters and showcases, and the outbuildings could hardly contain the overflow. I had a regular museum of more than five thousand items. Delegations, great crowds were coming all the time; I've had seventy-five and eighty people at once. I'd take them in groups all over the house, through each room, and lecture to them.

Finally in 1954 I started the Museum at Bridgewater College in Virginia. Ella and I spent months cataloguing 5,563 distinct items. That made four truckloads to cart the four hundred miles to Bridgewater. That got a big thing off my hands; but I still had so much stuff that I talked up enough interest around in the community, and we started the Jefferson County Historical Museum at the courthouse in Dandridge. I've been adding to both museums constantly all the time, and many other collections come in. People get teetery and tottery and begin to wonder what is to become of old things they have. And I get after them.

At Bridgewater I'm fixing to have a showcase labeled, *The Reuel B. Pritchett Museum Before 1900.* In that I'll have the bottle I cut my teeth on. My great-aunt Magdalene Sherfy gave it to my mother. I wore it tied around my neck with a string to chew on to get my teeth through. All us children used it, and then they lost it. When I was a good big boy, Daddy plowed it up in the garden, and I cabbaged on to it.

Also in that Bridgewater showcase I mean to have an oversize marble as big as a small apple, with stripes going from pole to pole in twisted form. And there'll be a two-cent piece. I owned a broken thermometer and traded it to a boy for the two-cent piece. He had a hankering for the thermometer and offered me the coin. I kept it all my life, and it's now in the museum. But the boy had bad luck with the thermometer. The bulb on the bottom you could pinch and see the column rise; take your fingers off and it'd slack. Well, to make it really rise he stuck it in a steaming teakettle and shot the top right off.

I live in Davy Crockett country. Davy used to go bear-hunting through here with his bear dogs, Blood, Death-Maul, Lightning, Thunderbolt, Tiger, and Whirlwind. Two and a half miles from my home, at Findlay's Gap, Davy met Polly Findlay, one of the first belles that Tennessee ever hatched. Davy got more interested in her even than in bearhunting, and she became his wife. The hearthstone and the foundation stones of the house where Polly grew up are still over there in Findlay's Gap. The house was tore down about fifty years ago, and the man built a barn with the logs. We've been trying to create enough interest to rebuild that cabin over the same foundation and hearthstone, using the same logs.

The house I live in is a relic and a monument. It is the old Benny Carson home, situated on the old Chuckey Road, once the stage road. Said to be the first frame house outside the town of Dandridge, it was built in 1845, the same year as the courthouse in Dandridge. In about 1921 I held a revival down here at the French Broad church. They called me to come and be pastor. I found out this farm was for sale. I liked the church and liked the country purty well, so I sold my land on Knob Creek and bought this farm.

This section of Tennessee was on the border between the North and the South. The armies shifted to and fro across it. On December 24, 1863, the Battle of Dandridge was principally fought, though there followed a series of skirmishes for a month afterward. Soldiers first of one side and then of the other would hunt cover in this house. In the wintertime they resorted to the cellar at the far end where they was very careless building big open fires. Benny Carson'd set up night after night to be sure the house wasn't burnt down by the soldiers. Fire did blaze up so much that it burnt a number of sleepers to a hull and charred the floor almost through. In 1925 I replaced the burnt sleepers and laid a new floor. But I kept some of the plank as a souvenir of that occasion. Still in the house from those days is a secret money drawer, a secret little small cellar for hiding food from the foraging soldiers, and a row of portholes for firing at the enemy through.

But most notable of all is the wide blood stain on the front room floor. Benny Carson's daughter, Mrs. Owens, visited me various times at the old homeplace. She told in particular how the

Carson children would never forget the screams and mourns that went up from a poor man as they were cutting his arm off without an anesthetic of any kind. Soldiers passed by on the old Chuckey Road for a couple of days and nights. A soldier stopped in who was gravely sick with a badly infected arm that had been shot in battle. Mr. Carson took care of him and waited a few hours till the doctors came along; they were in the rear. Mr. Carson summonsed them in. They examined the man and decided that his arm would have to be amputated. However, they didn't have the suitable tools and certainly no anesthetic.

They stopped a few soldiers, and in the Carson front room they put a man to hold each of his feet to the floor, one to set on his head, and one to grip the other arm. The doctors borrowed a butcher knife from the Carson kitchen and cut the man's arm down to the bone above the elbow. They borrowed a common saw and sawed off the bone. Then they pulled the skin down over and tied it, like tying a bag. The victim stood it and lived through it. He stayed with the Carsons a while, then went away. Mrs. Owens didn't know his name nor which army he belonged to or where he headed for. But she and the other Carson children could never erase from their minds the screams and mourns and shrieks of that man during the cutting and sawing. Blood from the operation covered the front room floor a couple of feet square and can still be seen, though I tried to cover it with a reddish paint. I've heard it said that you can never get a blood stain out of wood.

A colporteur was selling books, and my father bought a book called *The Golden Way*, autographed it, and gave it to me on January 1, 1890. It had 606 pages of choice sayings, good poems, famous pictures, and the cream of literature. Over my lifetime since then I've had a passion for books—scarce books, rare books, antique books, heirloom books owned by famous men, incunabula. The accumulation of books have mounted up to great proportions; I have more than three thousand volumes, most of which you'll hardly find anywhere else. I've picked them up here and yon, books that were printed when the railroads were shooting through the West and long before.

To hunt down rare books you've got to be able to follow a track just like a hound chasing a rabbit through a briar patch. He knows every turn the rabbit makes almost before he makes it. I uncover a clue and write somebody a letter of inquiry. I'm all a-tremble until an answer arrives back. But maybe the person is so slothful and lax that he doesn't answer. In such cases I write him a second letter and mail it to the same town c/o The Cemetery. That usually evokes a response.

The most valuable item I've ever collected is a Venice Bible printed in 1482, ten years before America was discovered. Martin Luther hadn't been born yet. It's vellum-bound, three volumes, 2700 pages, not a torn page in it, and gold leaf title letters two inches square laid in gold just like you'd fill your teeth with. I have it in a case made of mahogany logged in Africa by elephants, floated down the Congo to the seacoast, and shipped on to Charleston. Its cash value has been estimated at no less than $10,-000 and on up to $40,000. There's only five copies of the Venice Bible in the whole world.

My biggest obsession, though, has been for books from the five early American presses—from Christopher Sauer's press, Christopher Sauer, Jr.'s press, Peter Leibert's press, Samuel Sauer's press—those were all Dunkers—and from Ben Franklin's press. I quiver in my boots every time I get near a volume from one of those presses. The 1743 Sauer Bible printed in Germantown, Pennsylvania, by Christopher Sauer, Sr., was the first Bible printed on American soil in any European language. In 1763 Christopher Sauer, Jr., printed a second issue of the Sauer Bible. Before the 1776 issue he advertized the Bible to see how many people would want it. But between the time he advertized and the time he was going to print them, Ben Franklin got a corner on the paper and on the ink. So Sauer made his own paper and made his own ink. He gethered lampblack right out of his chimley, added some ingredients, and concocted a better ink than Ben Franklin could import. Two hundred years later Franklin's print is pale and Sauer's is bright.

There wasn't another European language Bible printed in America besides the Sauers' until some man in 1782 managed to get a subsidy from Congress and printed an English Bible. I've combed the woods all over the country for Sauer Bibles. Eight of mine are in the Bridgewater Museum.

Even scholars of research, as it happens, would never have heard of most of my books. Near Piney Flats, Tennessee, lived a man by the name of H. H. Hyder, who wrote two books. He was an eccentric; I knew him. One was a love story and I have that. The other has this title: *The Double Golden Chains with Blazing Diamonds Strung*. In the preface he relates how he had a vision one night, got up, wandered across the country two or three miles, set down on the bank of a creek in the moonlight with his feet dangling in the water, and when he came to himself, he returned to his home and wrote this book. He hadn't ever been to university or college, never had any education of any consequence, but he put up this most inspiring volume of poetry.

A few generations back there was considerable friction between the various Protestant churches in America. The Methodist Episcopal Church and the Missionary Baptists were great rivals in this country, and they spared no means one with the other in defense of their position. In 1855 a Missionary Baptist minister named J. R. Graves published a book titled

The

GREAT IRON WHEEL;

or,

REPUBLICANISM BACKWARDS

and

CHRISTIANITY REVERSED

There lived in Knoxville a prominent, energetic Methodist named Parson Brownlow, and through more than five hundred pages Graves spared no means to assail Brownlow's position politically and religiously and to say anything he could derogatory to the Methodist Church.

Shortly thereafter the Methodist conference met to find a man who could answer Graves's attack. And they selected Parson Brownlow himself. The next year he came out with a book titled

The

GREAT IRON WHEEL EXAMINED;

or,

ITS FALSE SPOKES EXTRACTED,

And

AN EXHIBITION OF ELDER GRAVES, ITS BUILDER

In a Series of Chapters

The two preachers laid each other and his religion out. I procured the opposing volumes fifteen hundred miles apart, and I don't know where else in the wide world except my library that you would find Graves and Brownlow side by side together.

I doubt if there's anybody else in the whole United States that's gone to so much trouble to have scrapbooks as me. I've spent four-fifths of a century drawing together ideas and facts that would otherwise have been lost. There's so much to investigate and preserve and examine and explain. The program is so big and life so short and there's so colossally much to be done that I can only scratch the surface of the things I'd like to see wound up before I have to go. History is always getting away from us. I see so much negligence and neglect, so much left undone, so many, many things that somebody ought to have taken care of and they didn't, and now it's too late.

Through the years when the children were home, they'd be trompling all over my toes asking for a drink or a piece of bread. Evenings we'd set around the fireplace. The children would go to bed earlier. Then Ella'd go. Everything settled into quiet, and the next couple of hours were my time for research, there by the little pile of embers. Later on I established a method of getting up at midnight after sleeping an hour or so. I jump out of bed regardless of the weather, fully dressed, do as much research as I can till I get drowsy. I've written hundreds of articles between midnight and 2 a.m. Ella used to tell our children, "You're sleepy. I'm gonna put you to bed." When I get drowsy, I say that to myself right out loud. I crawl in and take another nap.

I have thirty-five scrapbooks on various and sundered topics. A lot of it is classified; some is filed promiscuously under the title, *Odds and Ends and Clippings on Many Subjects*. I have scrapbooks or sections on such themes as midwives, catastrophes, centenarians, cruelty to children, boxing deaths, big trees, the Douglas Dam on the French Broad River, on and on, and of course my personal scrapbooks. Some go back more than half a century, and every clipping is dated. These scrapbooks are the main reason I get up each night. I'm possessed by them. I have thousands and thousands of clippings I haven't had time to file in my scrapbooks yet.

I've always been loath to have the house cleaned. Something gets broken every time. Irreplaceable information gets thrown away. Several years ago in cleaning house my helpers just dumped a whole pile of magazines into a box and set the box outdoors. Later it was stored on a back porch for a couple of years, nobody knowing but what it was discarded newspapers. On the wintry morning of December 18, 1963, I happened to probe into that box, and found the unclipped magazines I had never gone through, and thus retrieved a number of valuable articles, including a unique one on the Siamese twins, Chang and Eng.

It has been my lifelong habit never to throw a newspaper or magazine away till it has gone through my flint mill, even if it's a year old or more. In most families, if a newspaper comes at 6 in the morning, by evening nobody knows what's become of it. I don't know why they take it. For style I guess. A newspaper has little value that way.

I scan every headline, every byline. I read each article I care to read and clip every article I want to clip. On trains or buses or anywhere, I have hawk eyes for every newspaper lying around. Whenever I go to Washington, I can collect a good half a dozen papers from that many different cities. I've nothing else to do, so I run through the papers, take my penknife and cut out what interests me, widely respecting the margin and jotting the paper and date on the back. At my leisure I trim the clippings up, always leaving the little black line around it, and type in the identification and date.

I have two scrapbooks with the title

Child Marriage, Young Motherhood,

Multiple Births, twins, triplets,

Quadruplets, Quintuplets, Sextuplets,

or whatever number may be born at one time,

Identical twins, Siamese twins,

Monstrosity Births, Odd Marriages,

Wide Differences in Ages at Marriage.

There have been a number of quintuplets, but sextuplets are very rare. I have the clipping and picture of the greatest record we know anything about: a heathen woman somewhere across the water gave birth to ten babies at a single time. However, they all died.

Another two of my scrapbooks contain practically all my railroad and bus receipts and stubs for nearly fifty years. They represent more than 400,000 miles, and I haven't a one in there that I didn't ride. On the floor in a bus terminal or a railroad office I could pick up hundreds of stubs, but I never have, no matter how beautiful or well-preserved. I've only kept the ones that I rode. The Southern Railway Company would like to have these scrapbooks for their archives. They say they never heard of a scrapbook of travel stubs.

Many times I've made the acquaintance of people I kept clippings about. A man named Brinkley had the longest beard in the world. It stretched down to his feet; he could stand on it. I went around to his place in North Carolina. Home he was from traveling and was hoeing in his garden. He had his beard rolled up on a slab of cardboard and tucked in his bosom. But even his eyebrows were almost mustaches.

I have a large file of all the articles I ever read about Sergeant Alvin York of the First World War. I visited him one time soon before his death and had prayer with him in his room.

I've always been profoundly interested in elephants. I have files and files of facts on elephants. The gestation period is twenty months. A baby elephant at birth weighs from 250 to 400 pounds and suckles its mother for two years. They grow to be ten or eleven feet tall and weigh up to 12,000 pounds or more. In captivity they've been know to live a hundred years; in the wilds perhaps much longer.

I have a lengthy scrapbook section on executions of elephants. Four have been executed in the United States, one in Germany, and various ones in Africa. The most notable execution ever held was the hanging of "Murderous" Mary. It took place while I was still living on Knob Creek. Mary was one of the largest and best-trained elephants in captivity. But an elephant, scarcely knowing its strength, can be highly dangerous. On September 12, 1916, during a performance at Kingsport, Tennessee, of the Sparks Circus, Mary slew her keeper, Mr. Eldridge. Some authorities say it was the seventh man, others the eighth man, killed by Mary. The state authorities demanded that Mary be tried, and the show consented. Lawyers went before a magistrate and presented the evidence. The magistrate passed a death sentence on Mary.

But the problem arose how to carry out the sentence. A well-aimed bullet right in the heart or brain won't kill an elephant quick. He may go on a wild vicious rampage before he dies. In Erwin where the show was to be the next day the circus people secured a railroad derrick and fixed on a location outside of town with a sink hole right beside the tracks. They put a team of men in there to dig it out more.

The execution was advertized for the afternoon. The showmen well knew they couldn't take Mary to the hanging ground by herself. They had to fool Mary, so they marched the whole herd of elephants out the couple of miles and maneuvered them in around the fresh grave. The derrick was swinging high above the scene, and a railroad hostler gently looped its chain around Mary's neck, without her knowing what they were up to. Then they started driving the other elephants back toward the showground. One bull elephant got suspicious. He headed down an alley, overturned a couple of little houses, scared a lot of people. A general stampede was barely avoided. But the attraction of the other elephants lumbering on down the street overpowered him, and he rushed on back to them, and they all went in the corral.

When the other elephants were all safely in the corral where they couldn't hear nor suspicion anything, the huge derrick begun to lift its unusual load. Mary kicked and jerked and lunged. She was hardly off of the ground when the chain broke, and she fell pell-mell. A furious battle would have ensued except that Mary was so dazed they got the chain keyed together and around her neck again before she could struggle to her feet. The derrick hoisted her again and "Murderous" Mary hung until she died. She was let down in the sink hole. They shoveled in the dirt and buried her there.

At the time there was a considerable barrage of criticism by Northern newspapers accusing Southern citizens of barbarous cruelty to dumb animals. Southern writers rallied to defend the action. I have that debate on file.

A decade later I contacted Major Pettiplace, the supervisor of the Clinchfield Railroad, and proposed that we exhume Mary's carcass, mount the bones, and exhibit them in some museum. He kindly consented and offered his section men to do the digging. But to our sorrow we discovered that the low place had been filled in and a railroad spur laid right across the grave. Consequently we were thwarted. Mary's bones rest in peace except for the whistle of the locomotives and the rumble of the long coal trains.

Prodigious facts like this from my own experience and out of the newspapers I have vast quantities of. But what's to become of them when I'm gone? Or does it make any difference? Maybe my executor will have the biggest bonfire there's been in East Tennessee for a long while. So few people have interest in history and preserving the past. Sometimes you feel you're in such an insignificant minority that you're crazy after all.

Chapter Sixteen

A MUSEUM FOR RELICS AND ANTIQUES

We advance so fast that antiquity gets behind—and antiques come into being. An antique ought to be treated as an antique. It is worse than a tragedy to try to concoct a desk lamp out of a coffee mill, or a news stand out of a baby cradle, or a dining room table out of a square piano. Some people mongrelize everything. The proper and safe place for relics and antiquities is in a musuem. To give an inkling of how inclusive and varied a museum can be, I'll list here a sample cross-section of some of the effects I have in the Reuel B. Pritchett Museum at Bridgewater College.

A brass medal in honor of John Tyler, President of the U.S.

A Malony Bros., Telford, Tenn., brass token: "Good for 5 cts in merchandise."

A stone celt found in the pocket of Jim Parks, eighty years old of Waynesville, N.C., after he burned to death in a strawstack near Dandridge, Tenn., on highways 25 and 70, March 12, 1936.

An effigy feminine head and face dug up in the grading at the Oak Ridge, Tenn., Atomic Energy Plant 1945. A man running a bulldozer saw it tumbling in front of his machine and sent it to me.

A most historic clock, gift to President William Howard Taft by the Prince of Wales, before his short reign as George VI.

A solid brass letter opener made from cartridges by a soldier in France during World War I.

Iron curling irons used by stylish girls in colonial days.

My grandfather's shoe last engraved: "D.B. 1850."

Elder John Bowman's long-handled set of waffle-irons, more than a hundred years old. Waffle irons are older than cookstoves. Put your dough for waffles, biscuits, cornbread, sweetcakes in there, close them like scissors, and bake it in the fire.

Twelve pairs of mussel shells from the St. Francis River, Arkansas, secured by RBP in person, April 1956.

A pale green pickle jar hauled in a wagon from Hawkins County, Tennessee, to Mentague County, Texas, by Elder Samuel Molsbee in 1888 and brought back to Tennessee by Elder Reuel B. Pritchett in 1939. (Sam and Abe Molsbee were two of the biggest preachers in all this country. They were identical twins, and if you weren't watching close, one could sit down and the othern get up to preach and you wouldn't know they'd changed. They buil identical brick houses on opposite sides of the road up in Hawkin County and could keep sixty and seventy people all night.) Th pickle jar is in the museum.

An over-size Coca Cola bottle made by the company as an ad vertisement on Dec. 25, 1923; 29 inches high. An average siz Coca Cola bottle 12 inches high. A miniature Coca Cola bottle 1/2 inches high.

A piece of shrapnel and three battered Minie balls from th battle of Antietam, picked up near the Dunker church, which wa shot through and through with cannon balls and grapeshot.

A tin metal torch arranged on a wooden handle so as to oscil late, used in an ovation in Greeneville, Tenn., Andrew Johnson' home town, to honor him on his being elected to the vice presidency; secured from an old man who took part in that ovation.

A collection of forty-one drafts for weaving. The draft wa drawn on a piece of paper, laid before the weaver, and used in similar way as the scale of music by a student playing the piano Most of the drafts were quite crude, but an expert weaver coul size up a pattern and know how to proceed. These are from 1835 an later, and have such names as: Tennessee Beauty, Rose and Lemon Worlds Wonder, Days Delight, Pine Top, Leaf and Snow Ball, Nin Snow Balls, Doors and Windows, Cluster of Vines.

The weaving collection at Bridgewater is the best one I know of in the United States. I've journeyed long distances over hills and up trails to acquire accessories pertaining to the weaving industry. Hardest to come by is the flaxbreak. They almost all got discarded because, being some six foot long and thirty inches high, they took up so much room. After the flax plant has been harvested and is sufficiently "rotted," it is run through the flax-break. One man operates a lever which chomps the upper breakers down on the lower ones. Another man feeds in the bundles of flax and the woody stems are broken up into "shives" or "shoves." The contraption was so homely and unsightly that it was dubbed "the clown of the loom house," and there was a common saying, "You're as awkward as a flax-break."

Terms from the weaving industry were a notable part of the language. My grandfather, when I was naughty, he used to say, "Reuel, if ye don't behave yerself, we'll give ye a good scutchin'." A wooden paddle with a sharp edge was used to scutch the shives off of the flax.

Many of my affects have a long and zigzagging history behind them. Take a big brass kittle in the museum at Dandridge. Over a hundred years ago, back when there was hardly anything like regulation of brewing liquors, the kittle was a distilling still. With the Civil War there arose a crying need for saltpeter or nitre to make powder out of. Some blacksmith cut the top off of this still, took a piece of copper and plugged up the hole in the side where the worm came out, riveted on ears and forged it a bail. All during the Civil War it was used to boil down heavily pregnant dirt into nitre.

Later it was purchased by the Government, and after that a well-to-do man owned it. He died, of course, and all his family died except one daughter that lived at home and used it as a wash kittle. When she died, her executor asked me to cry the sale. I used to do a lot of auctioneering. I sold the farm, sold the mineral rights, sold the affects. When we come to the old copper kittle, I cried and tried to get a bid. Only a low one came. I coaxed and got a slightly higher bid. For nearly all the people there it was nothing but a piece of junk. Finally I warned them, "If you don't want it, I'll sell it to the auctioneer. I raised the bid, give them plenty of chance, and cried, "Once—twice—thrice, and sold to the auctioneer."

I was driving a buggy with a spotted buggy horse. When I went to leave that evening after the auction, I crammed my buggy with all the things I could wedge into it, including myself; but there simply was no room for the big old whiskey still kittle. I drove on home, neglected to fetch it for three or four days, and when I returned, it was nowhere to be found. Aunt Anne Feltner was dead; the property was standing vacant; and somebody had carried away the kittle.

I did a bit of investigating and a couple of months later somebody give me an inkling as to what become of it. I drove to the house of a tenant farmer six or eight miles away. The fellow wasn't at home; nobody was. He had put the kittle to good use, had built a furnace in a little planked-up wash house to fit right around it. But there had come a cyclone and twisted that wash house around like a snail shell. My kittle was in the middle of that twisted, nailed, spiked, splintery mass. I chopped in with an axe, rescued the kittle, loaded it in my buggy and brought it happily home, Jefferson County Historical Museum in Dandridge, whereupon I donated it as a relic of the Civil War.

The first preacher of American Methodism was Robert Strawbridge, who emigrated from Ireland to Carroll County, Maryland, in the year 1760. In the year 1764 John and Elen Evans were baptized by him and became the first Methodist family in America (though some would dispute this). The old John Evans house, built in 1764, is still standing in Carroll County. Strawbridge often preached there and slept there. But nobody pays any attention to such historical monuments as this.

I was there investigating one day and crawled under the porch to get through the casement window. I peered into the cellar, and there was a family of skunks. There needed to be some yielding and concession on one side or the other, and I decided, after short deliberation, that it had better be me. But my heart was set on having some historical souvenirs from the house. The casement window had just been hewed out, and the mullions put inside of that. The frame and the four panes was in the act of falling out, so I picked up a piece of glass and a chunk of the casement wood, weaseled out from under the porch, and left this great Methodist shrine to the skunks.

I had a walnut frame cabinet made and deposited in it the chunk of wood, the pane of glass, and two Methodist disciplines. These mementos of Robert Strawbridge are now in the Seahorns Chapel Methodist Church, which crowns a hilltop about a half a mile from the French Broad church. *The Doctrines and Discipline of the Methodist Episcopal Church*, 1844, makes edifying reading for Methodists and Brethren yet today. Take in Chapter 2, Section VI:

"*Quest.* Should we insist on the rules concerning dress?

Answ. By all means. This is no time to give encouragement to superfluity of apparel. Therefore receive none into the Church till they have left off superfluous ornaments. In order to this, 1. Let every one who has charge of a circuit or station read Mr. Wesley's Thoughts upon Dress, at least once a year in every society. 2. In visiting the classes, be very mild, but very strict. 3. Allow of no exempt case: better one suffer than many. 4. Give no tickets to any that wear high heads, enormous bonnets, ruffles, or rings."

The Methodists lost that, and the other big churches. The Old Orders, the Amish, and the Yorkers major on it yet, farfetched though they are from everybody else. The Church of the Brethren held on in a casual way for a good while.

Chapter Seventeen

AN OCEAN-ROAMING COWBOY

I was once an ocean-roaming cowboy for horses. Several days after the close of World War II we set sea at New Orleans with 350 UNRRA (United Nations Relief and Rehabilitation Administration) horses and 10,000 tons of foods and feeds and relief goods to distribute in Greece. The name of our chubby freighter was the *Charles W. Wooster*. It was 485 feet long with a capacity of 10,500 tons, and we had it loaded to the hilt. The propeller on our ship was 18 feet in diameter and had a top speed of 71 revolutions per minute. Each time it revolved, it drove us 16 feet on our way. Our propeller turned over 2,379,572 times going across and 2,124,567 times coming back.

Dan West of the Brethren faith worked in Spain during Franco's insurrection and was permitted the privilege of helping on both sides. He saw that children and older people suffer the most of any citizens during a conflagration or war. He was frantically handing out powdered milk, which soon got all used up. Why not, he asked, bring over cows that would keep supplying milk? By the end of the fighting in World War II he was collecting a log of heifers and also calling for volunteer cowboys. I happened to be among the first volunteers. The Brethren made a contract with UNRRA and the United States government that we would help them take their horses over if they would let us have a ship to get our cargoes over. So our gang of cowboys went with horses, not heifers, and took orders from Washington when to go, where to stop, and where not to go.

I happened to be chosen captain of the sixteen men whose duties it was to take care of the horses. I wasn't supposed to work, but I worked all the time to keep the men a-working. Our ship wasn't built with horses in mind, and everything was unhandy. We had horses in the hull, in cages on the deck, even the upper deck, and in any corner we could find room to lodge one in. We fed them oats and hay twice daily, watered them in buckets that hung on the stable railings, and shoveled and windlassed and dumped overboard the old soiled bedding.

Horses get seasick sometimes, and when they do, they can become real maniacs. A horse'll reach around, grab another horse by the neck, bite out a piece as big as an egg, and leave the other horse a bloody sore. We'd have to tie the maniac down till he got better or died, whichever. But we only lost four horses as we was going over, the smallest percentage of any ship in the entire campaign. Every few days a colt would be born there on the rolling ship.

The *Charles W. Wooster* was a slow ship; we were twenty odd days reaching Greece. The last part of the trip was more dangerous because the Mediterranean Sea was lined with mines all along everywhere. The English furnished us a convoy; a couple of ships sailed ahead with a heavy cable strung between and hooks dragging down to ketch the mines. We stayed behind and between. All night we sailed and nothing happened. But at the peep of daylight a mighty explosion thundered through the ship. I raced to the top deck; smoke poured all around me. My final hour, though, had not yet struck. The English had snagged a mine just ahead of us and exploded it.

A horse boat a day or so ahead of us hit a mine. Ship, cargo, and all the horses perished at sea, though the men were saved. As we sailed into those waters, we could see a horse now and then swimming forlornly, a little out of sight of Thessalonika. Swim and swim they would till they gave out and yielded to the sharks.

In the harbor of Thessalonika the Greek government had arranged with the longshoremen to unload the horses. All we had to do was sit by and see it done. They had a big coop with bars at either end and they'd lower it onto the decks or into the hull. When the horse was in and the coop ready to be raised, I noticed that the longshoremen in their Greek dialect would shout, "*Mina, mina, mina, mina.*" I took over once in a while, and when a horse was ready, I'd holler out, "*Mina, mina, mina, mina!*" I didn't know what I was saying, but they laughed and gestured and raised the coop up just the same.

We had a corral made of ropes, provided with oats and hay. One old horse, as we were about to open the coop and let her into the corral, she surged against the bars, crashed through, buckjumped, and down the street she galloped. She was soon confronted by the sea wall. That horse was from Texas. She imagined she might get all the way back to Texas, maybe at one leap. Old Nell vaulted high, arched through the air, and hit the water ker-splash. Out through the harbor she started swimming.

Like any good harbor this one was a horseshoe with the corks close together. In its several hundred acres was twenty-three masts of ships sticking up that had been sunk during the war. Old Nell detoured around this ship and past that ship, skirted this wreck and that one. A couple of men got in a motorboat and started trailing her.

A horse swims deep. Just her nose and weathers is all that's out. She creates a lot of buoyancy and her abdomen'll hold her up. She doesn't have to make much effort; all four feet is down in there a-walking. She just paws and walks and travels. Old Nell made fine headway. She hit the horseshoe corks exactly, and on she swum right out into the deep sea. When the motorboat men got out past the corks, the sea was too deep for them and too wavy for them. They gave it up and turned back. But Old Nell was on her way to Texas. It wasn't but seven thousand watery miles, and she was willing to try it.

By midnight the horses were all unloaded, and we retired. The next morning, what do you suppose? Old Nell was with us again! She had decided Texas wasn't worth it after all. Back in from the deep dark sea she had swum, through the horseshoe corks and past the twenty-three sunken hulks. The tide was out, and there on a ledge of rocks next to the sea wall stood Nell, whickering and nickering to the horses in the corral. We went over with a winch, put a piece of gandy around the horse's middle, and windlassed her up. She seemed none the worse for her adventure except a wound on a hind leg where she must have struck one of the wreckages of a ship. Old Nell had a hankering for the corral this time and was soon munching her breakfast of oats and corn with the rest of the horses.

Wandering through the streets of Thessalonika, I saw a scene that can stand for a thousand other scenes. A bunch of girls and women were sitting on the ground around a spigot. It was not running a trickle of water as big as a pencil. They had little cups, gourds, or anything, each one trying to ketch a sip of water.

We visited dozens of ancient churches and castles, but I particularly recall the English Episcopal church. We went in, glad to be at some English service. The church was built dome-fashion, as has been the custom all over Greece. During the heat of the war it was used as a horse stable. Horses had been turned in this church and locked up. All the way around, up beyond the filth of the stable, high as a horse reach, the walls were all soiled. Around the dome was a row of windows, or had been. The mullions was still there, but every pane was blasted out. In front of the church were craters eight and ten feet deep. Only a few worshipers showed up that night. The boys and I from the boat helped make up the congregation. The usher was a hundred-year-old man.

The oldest denomination in the world that's still operating is the Greek Orthodox Church. In Thessalonika and Athens I visited ancient cathedrals so huge that a Brethren church here wouldn't make them a kitchen. And I had opportunities to meet a number of the Grecian priests. I could qualify with the priests because I wore a full beard, and they wore a full beard; they wore a mantle, and I wore a clergy. They put me in their class. I dined with them, I was in their homes, I was in their worships. They kissed me on the lips.

A priest invited me to go to a baptizing. That was right up my lane. I enjoyed it wonderful. Several husky men came with a huge laver big as a forty gallon apple kittle. They carried it on a pole through the ears and brought it right into the chapel. Six or eight priests were present and the secretaries and officers of the church. They poured in some water and had some ceremony. They poured in some oil and had some ceremony. There were ceremonies and more ceremonies. A lot of it was biblical. When all things stood ready, the priest drew me up to the edge of the laver where I could see what was going on, which pleased me greatly. The waiting child was eight or ten years old. And lo and behold, it was a triune immersion. I'm ignorant of Greek, but I could count. It was a pure unadulterated plunging face forward three times. It was a good mimic of the way we Brethren do it.

In Piraeus we dropped anchor along beside a destroyed seawall. Beyond it great sections of Athens were a shambles; almost every house was in wreck. There were no open streets; debris was everywhere. I scouted all over Athens for antiques. Bottle shops with their thousands of bottles kept luring me in. Uptown I saw some strange-shaped bottles of ink. I purchased the ink, stepped out to the curb, poured the ink in the gutter, and brought the bottle back to America with me. I liked the bottle better than the ink.

Off the main square in Athens, Constitution Square, I strolled into an antique shop crammed with fine distinguished articles. In America a dealer gets the trade through first. But not so in Greece. While I was fingering this old piece and that and we was starting to discuss a price, he ordered his servant out the door and down the street. The fellow returned with a pot of coffee and some little receptacles. We stopped trading. It was the thickest, syrupiest coffee I ever sucked into my mouth. The dealer kept dumping in refills, and we ate coffee. At length, with the pot emptied, we resumed our bargaining, and I negotiated several purchases.

He had, however, a copy of Gregorian chants hand-inscribed by an old sage on the isle of Athos several centuries before. Every monk is supposed to find a graduation project of some sort and follow it out. This old graduate decided he would make himself a volume of Gregorian chants. (The priesthood churches don't sing any hits or jazz but only music edited by the priests, which these chants were.) The monk tanned his own leather, spun his own thread, made his own paper, compounded his own ink. He did the whole job out and out. There's nary a press in America that could strike a line nor have uniform pages any more perfect than this hand-made creation of that graduating monk.

It became an heirloom in a family. But with hard times, war, and destitute circumstances, they took it down to this antique shop to sell it. The dealer's price was high. He showed it to me and admired it wonderful. But I walked out of the shop without it and headed toward Constitution Square, carrying what effects I had bought. The dealer, though, tagged along beside me. When I arrived at the underground train stop, I had a premonition. I said to the dealer, "Go back and fetch that Gregorian chant. I'm gonna take it." What a fool I'd almost been; halfway around the world and nearly missing the one chance to buy the only copy in the world.

He scurried back, wrapped the chant up in brown paper, and tied it with a string in every way. He boarded the train with me and we rode the fifteen miles to the Athenian harbor, where we had to take a motorboat to get out to the big ship.

It was some twenty feet from the water up to the deck of the *Charles W. Wooster*. I had an armful of stuff, and the dealer had an armful of stuff. He hired a boy to help us carry the things up. And, by Joe, if this boy didn't drop that Gregorian chant. It plummeted down between the motorboat and the big ship, and under the water it went. The water was all covered with scum and oil and grease of every kind; it was filthy. I nearly fainted: my precious, unique manuscript was sinking to the bottom of the briny sea.

But this dealer he scampered down the rope ladder, spotted the chant as it bobbed up, and raked it in. He slung the grease and filth and slime off of the wrapping, rubbed it off all over on his clothes. He hurried back up the ladder with the package, and we tore the string and paper off. So well was it wrapped that only at one corner had the water got in and made a few streaks. Otherwise it was all sound and safe. Were we elated! We had rescued an ancient treasure from the perils of the deep, thank the Lord.

I accompanied the chant book back to America. I don't know what it's worth, but I put it in the museum at Bridgewater.

We had orders to go from Athens to Naples and bring back as many soldiers as we could accomodate. We could see the lightnings flashing up out of Mt. Vesuvius when we were still forty miles away. It was hit and active but not running over. When we dropped anchor in Naples and had shore leave, I rushed like a crazy-man out to Pompeii. Of all the drunkenness and revelry and immorality, it was the center of the world of that time. Pompeii was the playhouse for all of Europe; it was the Atlantic City of the Roman Empire. No wonder God let it be destroyed. And it was such a complete job there wasn't anything lived: every louse and every insect, every reptile and rodent, and every last human being lost their lives in that storm of lava.

Naples itself was in purty bad shape; but wicked as the city was, full destruction had not yet been visited upon it. There were very few automobiles. Once in a while you'd hear the rough travel of a truck without any tires, just the rims on the hard brick. We were up and down the streets until 10 in the night. Many children went creeping around through the crowds. They didn't know where their parents were—dead or gone or missing. The little wretches, some of them as young as four years, were going all around begging for cigarettes or candy or anything to eat whatever. I've had many a child grab holt of my garments and cling tight till I'd have to pull his fingers loose a finger at a time, but I was without anything to give him. I had soap with me already and gave children a cake of soap, and they'd take the wrapper off and taste it. They had no idea it was not something edible; they had never once seen soap. The war'd been going on as long as they was old.

When the crowds thinned out, the children'd huddle themselves together in the entrances of old buildings and pile down for the night, all wore out, no cover for their bodies, no food for their shriveling stomachs. Nobody knew who was with him; they were all strangers to one another. A dozen or more of them would lay in the entrance of a storeroom, hungry, thirsty, dirty, unkept, and try to sleep a little before morning.

On our return voyage I made me a church on deck, right where one of the horse stables had been. I took a hose and flushed it all out nice and clean. It had open cracks like a crib. I got planks we'd used for partitions, scrubbed them all up, slipped them into the cracks, and made raised seats all the way back. I made me a stand and took a towel out of my grip for a spread on the stand. We was out on the deck, and the wind would be so heavy I'd have to weight the towel down with something, or my Bible and all would have been blown away. So I polished up some ammunition cartridges that I'd secured from under the rubble of waterfront warehouses in Athens and perched them on the spread for vases to hold it down tight.

There we would have open forum. We discussed everything. We had a big time. And I would preach. (I had preached going over, too, but without the deck chapel.) I wore work clothes, but when I went to preach, I put on my clergy. I washed and dressed and appeared as stately as I knew how to do. I had the high-ranking officers and the reprobate old seamen and the soldiers we were hauling back instead of horses. They all came to church, and I unloaded on them. I preached with as much emphasis as I would anywhere. One profane old seaman he said to me, "Mr. Pritchett, this is the first time we ever had any religion on this boat."

Chapter Eighteen

THE END OF A BEGINNING

I'm not afraid to die, but I sure hate to leave. Through fifty-six years I've compiled two big scrapbooks of people who reached a hundred years or more. I'm eighty-one now. I won't make it. I tell friends of mine when I meet them, "God bless you; pray for me, and come to my funeral. I'm going to have it some of these days." The pale horse and his rider are galloping nearer. I'm soon to quit, bad as I hate to.

My thoughts are engaged about foreclosing everything. That is awesome to consider. Heavy on me is the responsibility of the various things I have tried to do and am trying to do and am too old and too weak and too inefficient now to get it all done. I don't know how long he wants me to live, but I know time's running out. It would take a mighty little clip to clip my thread. I'll soon have to cash my checks. And I've got so much to do and so many things to do that I'm in a perfect straight all the time trying to get them done. That's why I find it a shame to go to bed and lose all that good time. My affairs here are so cluttered and jumbled; I'm simply not ready for the trip. If the Lord will help me divest my mind of these temporal things, these files, collections, projects, if he'll get them out of the way, let me down easy, take the dread off, ah, that will be glorious.

I don't want a sedative on that day, none when I'm passing through the dark lane. I want to see what's going on down through there. If I'm gonna have a Companion—and the Book says he will be with me to the end—I want to talk with him and have his comradeship through the oracles of death.

I have a custom ever since the day Ella and I married; I try to have a family altar each night. I have it now just the same as if there was the whole family with me. Of course my family is near to me, all the members of my family. I'm not sure what the Lord thinks of my arrangement; it may look purty monotonous to him, but it is serious with me, and I ask him to be tolerant about it. I have a little prayer list in my mind. When I'm drowsy and sleepy and tired and worn out, I need to be purty brief, but I go through it anyhow. Hundreds of people ask me to pray for them. If I prayed for everybody individually and one at a time, I'd just be praying night and day I guess. I have to make it wholesale to some extent.

My prayer list has evoluted a lot. Back in my boyhood it was Father and Mother, two sisters and a brother, and me. That made six. I went down the line and rolled over each name, asking the Lord to bless them. But weighty changes came. Lizzie died and I checked her off; God would take care of her all right. Ella entered my life and went to the head of my list. A child was born and I included him. Another was born and another, and another, and I remembered each of them. My sister Claudie married, and I included her husband. My brother John married, and I included his wife. They had a son, and I added him, and later his wife and children. Father died, and I checked him off. Mother died, and I checked her off. That whole generation passed. My sister's husband died, and he was left off. Dr. Kintner married my daughter Ethel, and I included him. Now they have four children, and I include all of them. They had one child that didn't live more than a few hours. I checked it on and checked it off the same day. Erlene married, and I added her husband. Evelyn died, and I checked off my daughter, I checked off my own daughter. She died in childbirth, and the baby lived. I put him on the list as I was taking Evelyn off. Her young husband was on the list. My daughter Erlene's husband died, and I left him off. My wife Ella died, and I checked her off. I've checked off about as many as I've checked on. And soon God will check off my whole prayer list and me with it and take me where he can teach me to do the thing better.

Father died before Mother. They still lived on the old farm by Knob Creek. I had already moved to Jefferson County and the French Broad church. Daddy took a bad spell of sickness on the fifteenth day of March when he was seventy-nine years old and living in his eightieth year. That disease, whatever it was, affected his breathing and lungs. He couldn't lie down at night; he'd set up in a chair and sleep.

I went often to visit him. Father was more or less timid. He never talked much about death and funerals. When a death happened in the community, you could see that he was greatly affected. When death struck in our home, as with Lizzie and Grandfather Bowman, he was almost speechless. He'd walk around with nothing much to say or sit with his hands over his face and think. He was in a deep study—deeper of course when it was in his own home. But also, after a death in the community, his voice would grow strangely low and weak. You could see the sympathy flowing out of Daddy. He never said much about dying himself. But when he came to his own deathbed, he turned to me and sighed, "Reuel, this is it."

I said, "No, surely not, Daddy. It'll be all right."

"No," he said, "no."

He kept on arguing with me about this being the end, and I said, "Well, Daddy, if you must go, go ahead and tell 'em I'm a-coming."

His condition worsened. The fifteenth day of October, 1933, came. He got so weak he just had to lay back, and we laid him down gently. I sat at the side of the bed, and John was there too. I held his pulse as long as there was any pulse. When the pulse was gone, I put my fingers up under his chin and could feel the least little twitch of a pulse that could send a trickle of blood up that far when it wouldn't go down to the wrist. I touched that feeble pulse as long as it lasted. Daddy gasped a time or two, rolled back his eyes, and relaxed in death.

Seven years later Mother, she got terribly low. She was unconscious and didn't know what was going on. But after the elders anointed her, she revived out of that purty good for several weeks and got to where she could talk. "Reuel," she said, "this whole thing has to be gone through over again. I should have went on when I was nearly gone. I've got to die again." And so it was.

No death was ever so hard for me as my daughter Evelyn's death. It was the profoundest disappointment I have ever had to go through. It grates me still. She'd had two accidents: she had fell off of a bicycle, and the other was that a bad mischievious boy pushed her off of a porch at school, and she had to jump four or five feet. She lit on her feet, but her pelvis bone was damaged in both cases. When pregnancy came, there was an obstruction. The doctors tried to deliver the baby past the obstruction in the normal fashion, but there was no way to do that except to dissect the baby. They resorted to Caesarian section and tried to save them both, which according to medical science was almost impossible to do after all that went before. Evelyn lived a few days and during the first several days she inquired about the baby. The nurse would bring him in and show him to her. She'd smile, and a time or two she said, "It's worth it."

Evelyn was an exquisite Christian girl. She died at twenty-two. She and A. B. Watkins, her husband, were going to build a house about a quarter of a mile from us. They'd've been close by to help support the church and sort of look after Ella and me in our old days. But that all fell flat, all went to nothing.

If we recognize our loved ones in the great Beyond, I sure want to have a long association with that girl. What an old world of things and a new world of things we'll have to discuss.

Ella had arthritis for ten years and was an invalid five or six years. She was a good mother as long as she lived. Her faith remained strong all through her illness. I was her nurse. In her last days she was so helpless. She'd be awake in the night and call out,

"Help me, Reuel, help me." I lived and Ella didn't live. It's been now eight years, and it is not uncommon for me to have a dream or vision and hear her call out, "Help me, Reuel, help me." When I hear that in the night, I answer. That wakes me up, and it's a dream.

Whenever I arrived home from a mission off somewhere, Ella would meet me halfway down the steps. I'm looking forward soon again to being met by her halfway down the steps.

Ella lived above the average of her people. They don't live long. She died at seventy-two. Her mother died at fifty-six; her father at sixty-five. My father died at seventy-nine and my mother at seventy-nine; Father's mother at about sixty-five and his father at something under seventy. Mother's father and mother both died at sixty-eight years, one month, and twenty days. I'm eighty-one past. I have so far outlived any of them on either side, for which I'm most thankful. I'm like the old man who reached a hundred. Somebody shook hands with him and says, "I understand you're a hundred."

"Oh, yes," he says, "and I'm mighty glad of it."

"Mighty glad of it? What d'ye mean?"

"I'da been dead if I wasn't a hundred."

I don't have ancestors on either side that lived into their nineties or upper eighties. I'm the last one left. It's my turn. I'm next. It's my move on the checkerboard.

I am an extremely improbable individual. It was rare and unlikely that I got born to begin with. Grandfather James Pritchett was the weakest, smallest pattern in Great-grandfather Singleton's family. He had a brother John, and Hiter and Mark. His brothers were pressed into the Civil War and lost their lives. James was a weakling, almost an invalid. He remained home and didn't die. How was it decided, how was it determined, that Uncle Hiter's whole posterity would be cut off, and Uncle John's and Uncle Mark's, and that Grandfather James would be preserved and all his lineage, and that through this medium I would be permitted to live? How was God in that? I don't know. But this I do know, that I owe God more than I can imagine for being able to perceive, comprehend, enjoy—*live*. How wonderful it is to grace God's earth!

How can we pay so little attention to living? Once when I was surveying the grandeur of Niagara Falls, a freight train came along near the foot of the Falls. On a boxcar sat a boy with his back turned to the mighty cataract. He was facing the drab cliff on the opposite side and never once looked around. How can we be like that to life?

Three human beings are born with the tick of every second.

Near two hundred thousand of our fellows die every day. An unending belt carries the generations in and out of time and on into the stretches of eternity. My generation, I've seen them one by one be carried past the dark bend in that belt. In God's Word sand and stars and angels and men are innumerable. The sands of the sea or a skyful of stars may pass away, but of the innumerable human multitude pouring in on the eternal shore not one will be blotted out. Now is the day of salvation. The day of this world is far spent; it's after milking time on the clock of history.

They used to sing a song that the storms will soon be over. I didn't know they were talking about the storms of time; I thought they meant the actual dark raging winds. When a black storm came up, I was wondering, Are we going to have one more? Many and mighty are the storms that have surged upon us. But they will all be over directly. The final storm is soon to rage near and be gone, the ultimate thunder, the last lightning.

Death is the end of a beginning. Death is commencement in eternity. What will we be like strolling through the halls of eternity? "It doth not yet appear what we shall be." But we'll be like him, like Jesus. He rose in glorious body. He was white as the light; he shined like the sun. We'll behold his glory and share it. That's plenty to know about our coming life.

Suppose I'd say to an old green tobacco worm, treacherous-looking little critter: "Tomorrow you'll spin a cocoon with a thousand silk threads, and in a few weeks you'll cut out with beautiful downy wings, float in the wind overhead of everything, and sup the nectar from ten thousand flowers, whereas now you're squirting this old green tobacco juice."

Suppose I take an egg that's just beginning to pip. I hold it to my ear and listen to the life in it and say to that egg, "Tomorrow, little chick, you'll crack the dome of this home of yours, crawl out under the vast dome of heaven with your mates and see God's sunshine." He can hardly have an inkling of what's about to be.

Or the little chimley swift, born and bred and raised down in the flue of a dark chimley. Suppose I'd say to the frail creature, "Tomorrow you'll rise up out of this old sooty narrow place. You'll spread your wings and skim wide and far under the radiant blue of heaven." He wouldn't understand. Down in there he can see only a sliver of sky.

I'm the worm, the egg, the chimley swift. We all are. Jesus tries to tell us what we're to be. We can't comprehend. But through a glass darkly we see him that we're to be like. Marvelous beyond belief has it been to grace God's earth, this waiting room to eternity. What will it be like to grace the strands and slopes of heaven?